Can Artificial Intelligence and Big Data Analytics Save the Future of Psychiatry?

Can Artificial Intelligence and Big Data Analytics Save the Future of Psychiatry?

The Search for a New Psychiatry
and Other Challenges

A. George Awad

CAN ARTIFICIAL INTELLIGENCE AND BIG DATA ANALYTICS SAVE THE FUTURE OF PSYCHIATRY? THE SEARCH FOR A NEW PSYCHIATRY AND OTHER CHALLENGES

iUniverse books may be ordered through booksellers or by contacting:

iUniverse
1663 Liberty Drive
Bloomington, IN 47403
www.iuniverse.com
844-349-9409

Because of the dynamic nature of the Internet, any web addresses or links contained in this book may have changed since publication and may no longer be valid. The views expressed in this work are solely those of the author and do not necessarily reflect the views of the publisher, and the publisher hereby disclaims any responsibility for them.

Any people depicted in stock imagery provided by Getty Images are models, and such images are being used for illustrative purposes only.
Certain stock imagery © Getty Images.

ISBN: 978-1-6632-5267-8 (sc)
ISBN: 978-1-6632-5268-5 (e)

Print information available on the last page.

iUniverse rev. date: 04/24/2023

CONTENTS

Part B2: Clinical Challenges

Part C: Conclusion

DEDICATION

To my wife, Lara, and our son, Michel, for their valuable encouragement and support. Lara's engineering skills, plus her extensive astronomical knowledge and her futuristic expertise has added value and guided the development process of this manuscript. Our son, Michel (Michael, as he is better known), has enhanced this book with his advice and expertise in the arts and design, in the preparation of the front and back covers, as well as all the pages in between. Thanks, Michel.

ACKNOWLEDGEMENT

As in previous books, I am indebted to Ms. Pamela Walsh for her valuable and competent assistance in the preparation of the manuscript for this book, from my own scribbles to a much better and more readable text. It is a skill that has added clarity and value. Many thanks, Pam.

Just before spring thaw-by the author AG Awad,
Oil on Canvas,14"x14",1974

FOREWORD

George Awad is a physician with a unique history: Childhood and medical school in Egypt followed by general practice in a small village, a PhD in pharmacology in Moscow, then a stint in Italy to study cardiovascular response to stress, followed by immigration to Canada. He was doing an internship in Toronto to qualify for practice in Canada and I, a local boy, was doing a rotation in general surgery as part of my neurosurgical training. How lucky for me that we wound up at the same hospital. In this book, Dr. Awad writes about the age that we are all entering in which artificial intelligence (AI) will alter every aspect of human endeavor. He describes the historic disconnect between brain sciences and the mind, as represented by behavioural neurology with its emphasis on how physical disease alters behaviour, and psychiatry which has mostly relied on the observation of human behaviour without reference to the physical brain. Since the advent of chlorpromazine in the 1950s, the first widely used psychotropic medication, there has been considerable effort given to elucidating the effect of altered brain chemistry on emotion and cognition from the psychiatric side. Dr. Awad has participated in the exploration of the mind brain connection over a lifetime of clinical practice and clinical trials of psychotropic medication. He has been a leader both in the organization of scientific investigation and the quotidian delivery of individual psychiatric care.

I can think of no better guide to follow into this brave new world.

Michael Louis Schwartz
Professor, Department of Surgery
University of Toronto, Division of Neurosurgery,
Hurvitz Brain Science,
Sunnybrook Health Science Centre
Toronto. Canada

INTRODUCTION

The Continued Search for a New Psychiatry

This book is the second of my recent series about the search for a new and stronger psychiatry. The first book of this series was published in 2021, with the title "The Search for a New Psychiatry – On Becoming a Psychiatrist, a Neuroscientist and Other Fragments of Memory". The idea behind last year's book was to review both the historical development and the current state of psychiatry, written as a biographical sketch of my own experiences over the past sixty years, which in reality almost corresponds to the development of modern psychiatry itself, from the 1940s onward.

What quickly became clear was the uneven state of progress in psychiatry, with a few short peaks of optimism and scientific progress, separated by lengthy periods of stagnation and dominated by low or no progress. The initial progressive period in the 1940s and early 1950s was boosted by the major development of the antipsychotic Chlorpromazine and a few other similar medications, the introduction of new and more specific antidepressants, and all augmented by the gradually waning state of the psychoanalytic dogma that dominated the field for several decades prior.

It wasn't long before this optimistic and progressive phase was tempered by the recognition of the various limitations of the new class of antipsychotics. Not only did Chlorpromazine and related medications prove to be not fully effective against the broad spectrum of psychotic symptoms in schizophrenia, but also by the emergence of frequent serious side effects, undermining compliant behaviour. Nevertheless, the introduction of this class of medications, though not fully effective, facilitated the precipitous discharge of chronic psychiatric patients from psychiatric asylums to a community that was not welcoming, nor able to support them. It was a move that crippled the proper organization of psychiatric services for a long time to come. The rapid and inadequately prepared shift from the asylum to the community may have hastened the demise of the dreadful mental asylums and quickly led to a clearly fragmented model of care that was generally of poor quality and lacked effectiveness.

Such was the state of psychiatry in the 1970s, with no one seemingly satisfied. Patients continued to struggle with treatments that proved to be, at best, only partially effective, and they experienced serious side effects. Families were burdened by frequently having to assume the role of caregivers, and doctors felt limited by unmet needs, both in science and clinical practice. Several commissions, task forces and major reviews were established, but their efforts proved to be no more than tweaks, as it became clear that pouring funds into a broken system produced no significant reforms. Though advances in medical technology in the late 1980s had provided exceptional opportunities for psychiatry by the introduction of neuroimaging technology, it was quickly limited by the absence of further technological improvement. In the end, though pockets of progress managed to continue, it was too little and too slow to satisfy patients and their doctors, who still continue to be burdened by the lack of backing by strong science and practice in a poorly funded and fragmented clinical service model. That was my conclusion in the 2021 book.

In other words, the 2021 book provided the imperative for the search for a new psychiatry that would secure a better future, which is what I am hoping to provide through this book, by exploring a role for the application of new informatics technology. It has already proven to be helpful in several other medical specialties, as well as in many aspects of our daily life. I recognize that employing information technology is not the only path for the future, but certainly it is one of the few paths that has demonstrated its positive potential. Though it is a path that has never been fully explored, it has already contributed many benefits to medicine. I have to admit that when I started composing the manuscript for this book, it was with my eyes wide open to the low interest among psychiatrists to incorporate technological advances in the practice of psychiatry, and the erroneous excuse of losing empathic psychiatry. This excuse is basically erroneous, as information technology is just a tool that can proceed, with all its algorithms, under full human control.

Now, as I complete this book manuscript, I have no hesitation in strongly recommending a path of modern informatics as a potentially strong approach to better secure the future of psychiatry. I am truly gratified by the recent decision this spring by the Royal College of Physicians and Surgeons of Canada to endorse its council recommendations concerning the integration of information technology and digital approaches in medicine, as well as specialty training. To me, it is more than just an important endorsement for mapping the future of medicine, but also a vote of confidence and validation for my early choice of such an important topic as the central theme of this book.

The book is organized in three main parts; Part A deals with the many aspects of the evolving subject of information technology, which has given the book its title. Recognizing the low interest of this topic among psychiatrists, as documented in one of the chapters, I attempted to simplify the provision of the various complex technological information available. I, myself, have to admit that I do not possess high technological knowledge or skills, but I am approaching complex technological issues from the perspective of a clinician and neuroscientist. The first few chapters document the successful story of developing a Covid-19 vaccine in a relatively short time, based on the use of the new science of mRNA and information technology, that includes artificial intelligence and big data analytics. These major successful scientific and medical technologies gave me the clear notion of whether such an effective and expedient approach could be applicable to psychiatry in moving rapidly to a more secure future. Part A also includes a summary of the development and application of the new pharmacogenomic information already accessible and its potential contribution to the development of precise psychiatry, matching treatment to the individual patient at the right time. At the end of Part A, I provide my response to the big question: Can artificial intelligence and big data save the future of psychiatry? My answer is yes, I think it can.

Part B includes a number of clinical and controversial challenges grouped under two headings that include phenomenological and nosological challenges and clinical controversies, based on my long clinical and academic practices. The topics covered include the recent development in neurology of the new discipline of behavioural neurology and the challenge of neuropsychiatry, and the subjective/objective dichotomy in psychiatry. Other clinical challenges and controversies include topics such as loneliness and its role as a silent and invisible disorder, and the reemergence of psychedelic drugs and their future in psychiatry and several other clinical challenges.

Part C provides conclusions, selected bibliography and a postscript that was hastily included, as a tribute to the memory of Professor Thomas Arthur Ban. Tom, as he preferred to be called, who sadly died recently, in February of this year, was a major loss of a genuine and dear friend. He was a pioneer of the science of modern neuropsychopharmacology and a true humanist who cared and helped many others.

Overall, I am delighted to share my thoughts with the readers towards the goal of creating a conversation that can further the future of psychiatry.

A. George Awad
Toronto, Canada 2022

PART A

Can New Information Technology Save the Future of Psychiatry?

Starting From Where I Stopped

About three years ago, I entertained the notion of developing two manuscripts for two books that would mark my pending retirement, after almost seventy years of an academic medical career that started in 1949 as a medical student at Cairo University, in Egypt. Such a long career seems to have coincided with the history of modern psychiatry, which had its beginnings in the 1940s. I decided that one of the books would be about neuroscience, in which I had been educated and had practiced across three continents; in Cairo, then Moscow, back briefly to Cairo, then on to Rome and eventually to my final destination in Toronto, Canada.

My seven years of medical studies in Cairo turned out to be one of the most exciting periods of my life. I cherished my independence, living away from the family, and wisely spent that time attending to my studies, as well as enjoying the opportunity of living in an ancient historical city like Cairo. I quickly discovered that Cairo was not one city, but several cities bound together by a veneer of modernity. There was "Islamic Cairo", "Coptic Cairo" and "Jewish Cairo", all distinct by their unique architecture and the way of life that marks its origins in the many dynasties that ruled Egypt. Through numerous visits to these unique districts, I became more acquainted with our ancient history. Not only did it provide knowledge, but also put me in touch with parts of myself that enhanced a feeling of identity, irrespective of identification with any organized formal religions or philosophies.

Unfortunately, early on I developed a clear antipathy to psychiatry, following an observation of live sessions of insulin coma therapy, which looked somewhat cruel and barbaric and left me feeling that the treatment was worse than the illness itself. My antipathy became accentuated by my obligatory clinical training visits to an ancient mental asylum, with a history that goes back to the eighth century. Though the old designation of the Cairo Lunatic Asylum had been changed in recent years to "psychiatric hospital", it continued to suffer from overcrowding and under-funding. Yet, its fascinating ancient history focused my interest on the history of mental healthcare in Egypt, that preceded any such efforts in Europe by developing the earliest concept of a mental asylum in the Cairo of the eighth century. I became aware of what was known as "colonial psychiatry", that referred to the era of the British occupation of Egypt from 1882 to 1954, during which the British authorities took charge of the mental asylums in Egypt. It was clear that the British authority may have improved the system of management, but they introduced no science and may have deliberately delayed the development of academic psychiatry in Egypt, likely for self-serving reasons.

Throughout my seven years of medical studies, I witnessed political chaos that created a good deal of major events that impacted and shaped my thinking. Numerous protests and demonstrations led to rapid government changes, political assassinations, repression and widespread arrests. The humiliating defeat of the Egyptian army in the battle of Israel's War of Independence in 1948, followed by the grand Cairo fire in January 1952 that destroyed the commercial core and all foreign-owned properties, triggered by violent miscalculations of the British occupying authority, led to the July 1952 army revolution that toppled the monarchy. On and on went the relentless life of turmoil in Cairo, which was not only distracting, but also illuminated the powerful impact of repression, poverty and social upheaval.

To make matters and life in Egypt much more complicated, in 1956, the year my medical class was to graduate, a major international crisis erupted, with its centre in Alexandria, Egypt. There, in a fiery and combative speech, President Nasser announced his retaliative response, to nationalize and take over the full control of the Suez Canal, which had been mostly run by a French and British consortium since it opened for navigation in 1869. In no time, Nasser's abrupt take-over decision managed to anger western countries, particularly in the case of France and the United Kingdom, who had managed and controlled the operation and revenues from the vital marine link. Nasser's motives were clearly understood as a retaliation after western countries decided to withdraw their financial and technological support for the development of the high Aswan Dam in Upper Egypt. It was the central plank of Nasser's plans to revive the depressed agricultural economy and provide more energy supply to the vast countryside outside of the big cities.

Meanwhile, the equally angry France and United Kingdom managed to secretly hatch a plan to retake control of the Suez Canal by force, aided by the willingness of the Israeli army to participate in the secret invasion plans against their political foe and major critic; President Nasser. By October 1956, Israel's troops marched through the Sinai Desert, approaching close to the eastern banks of the Suez Canal, while the British and French navy ships were already blocking the Mediterranean entrance of the Canal, a move that threatened and angered many of the protesters in major capitals of the world who were worried about the return of the dreaded colonial era. Angry about not being informed of the secret plans of the invasion with the potential for a bigger war engulfing the unfriendly western and eastern political blocks, the United State's government condemned the tripartite invasion and joined the international pressure for a cessation of the hostilities and the full withdrawal of the invading forces.

Egypt was pressured to compensate international shareholders of the seized Anglo-French Suez Canal Company, in return for Egypt's full control of the Canal and its revenues, with the condition of Egypt guaranteeing the rights of navigation for all countries. On balance, then, Egypt has been considered the winner of this major and costly conflict, while the British Prime Minister Antony Eden was seriously criticized and censored by the British parliament and eventually forced to resign.

For me and for all Egyptians, life slowly returned to its regular but rather noisy and overcrowded pattern. Eventually the generally subdued and postponed graduation ceremonies took place in January 1957, and in a couple of weeks mine and all our classmates' minds were each mostly focused on the early beginning of our independent medical career at the end of the year of further training as a house officer, the British equivalent of an internship in the US medical system.

Completing my house officer's year, my first independent job as a rural physician was a challenge, serving a remote and poor area of Egypt close to the region of the Suez Canal, but provided valuable opportunities and experiences dealing with endemic pellagra and pellagra's madness. Within a few months of treating the nutritionally deficient and lethargic population with inexpensive brewer's yeast, it awakened the region and brought me an almost magical fame. It also introduced me to the first inkling of interest in the study of neuroscience as a career option.

By the end of three years, the time had come to prepare for my first trip abroad, having received a bursary by the government to support my graduate studies. It was originally planned to be in London, the traditional place for postgraduate training among Egyptian medical graduates, but there was a last-minute change of destination by the government that was blamed on the poor relationship between Egypt and the United Kingdom in the aftermath of the Suez Canal War in 1956. With no choice, I agreed to go to the totally unknown destination of Russia, and completely unfamiliar with the Russian language. But in the end, with my curiosity of the secretive and mysterious Soviet system and my fondness for Russian classical literature, I overcame any serious hesitation.

My trip to Moscow, or what I used to call my "expedition of discovery", turned out initially to be uncomfortable and challenging. Besides my studies, I had to deal with issues such as politics and ideology, and also with personal issues such as loneliness, trust, friendship and religion, or more precisely, the absence of it. Though I had been for years mostly neutral regarding anything religious, I found myself curious about an aspect that raised questions concerning the interface of science and religion, and whether science can progress and flourish in the absence of formal religion. By the end of almost four years in Moscow, I was clear on the answer to such frequently debated topic; sure, science can progress without religion, but at the same time, at least in the Soviet Union, the benefits from science did not extend to help the population outside of political and military uses.

My studies in Moscow focused on the most topical research and scientific concept at the time, "stress" and its impact on health and disease, as formulated by Professor Hans Selye at McGill University in Montreal, Canada. At that time, I reasonably guessed that every second or third PhD dissertation was based on an aspect of such a novel concept. My training, both research and clinical, was substantially facilitated by the trust and friendship that was extended to me by the staff of the Department of Experimental Endocrinology. The staff was comprised of forty-two female scientists, with only two men in the department; my supervisor and director of the department, and myself.

I returned to Cairo with my doctorate degree, as well as a wife from Kiev whom I had dated throughout my four years there. My return proved to be a major disappointment, related to my mis-appointment in a senior post that was mostly administrative, overseeing a program of the toxicological clearance of urgently imported grains. The grains would stay in the ships arriving at the Port of Alexandria until clearance was received after a random sample of grains was sent by express train to a laboratory in Cairo, where it was tested by using mice. Obviously, I quickly realized the process was primitive and open to corruption and politics. Any delay would create shortages of the government-subsidized bread, which meant the streets would fill with political demonstrators. Any effort to reform and modernize the system, or at least build the necessary laboratories close to the port in Alexandria, did not go anywhere.

The following three years in Cairo proved to be a waiting game to secure a scientific opportunity that would allow me to travel abroad. By the end of three years, I was ecstatic to receive an award for a post-doctoral year at the prestigious Health Research Institute in Rome, which guaranteed the Egyptian government's approval to travel to Rome. In Rome, I consolidated my research interest in the concept of stress, and managed to share a co-authorship paper of the project's results in one of the well-known medical journals. It also gave me the opportunity to freely decide not to return to my job in Cairo. Luckily, with some help, I managed to secure a training position in London's post-graduate clinic for further training.

However, in a switch of destiny, I never made it to London, as I had received an attractive offer for an academic post to develop a new laboratory for experimental neuroendocrinology in the newly opened medical school at the University of Calgary, in Alberta, Canada. I accepted the surprise offer, as I had been looking to finally settle down in one place that I could call my new home, not withstanding the expected Calgary harsh winter weather.

How all that took place was in reality a major surprise for me that I never contemplated nor planned. As happened, the Soviet Union marched its army to invade Czechoslovakia in the summer of 1968 to quell the democratic uprising in Prague, with the result of many citizens in Europe deciding not to return to their country. Among those was a radiologist from Prague who was our befriended neighbour and post-doctoral colleague at the same research Institute of Rome that I attended. He and his wife accepted an invitation from Canada to immigrate and settle there. Knowing my plan not to return to Egypt, he connected me with the professor of endocrinology in the newly-opened medical school at the University of Calgary, not far from where he had settled, working at Edmonton University.

Yet, in another twist of fate, I never made it to the city of Calgary. In a short stop-over for a few days in Toronto, Canada, on my way to Calgary, I briefly visited the University of Toronto, which to my surprise, ended with an offer of a research job in the Department of Pharmacology. I accepted the position, and without delay I started immediately to manage a long-stalled major thyroid research project. I enjoyed the friendly and very welcoming environment, which helped me to conclude the major multi-centre project and co-author a critical paper of the results, published in the prestigious medical journal The Lancet.

With my proven research capabilities backing me, I accepted an invitation to move to the Department of Psychiatry, which was in the midst of a major development of biological psychiatry. By 1974, I had my first independent job at the old Lakeshore Hospital in Toronto, which was noted to be a unique psychiatric hospital, having been built by its own patients. Shortly after, I was invited to move to the main psychiatric hospital, built in the 1850s and renovated several times, known as "999 Queen Street", being located at 999 Queen Street West in Toronto. It was there, during my tenure as the Psychiatrist Director of the south-western region of Toronto, that my full academic research contributions unfolded. It was also where I pursued my clinical and research interests on psychiatric disorders, with a particular focus on schizophrenia and the challenges experienced by the person behind the illness, as already detailed in part two of my 2021 book.

In part two, a brief review of my contributions were included, both clinical and academic, along with the accomplishments and missed opportunities. I assumed several senior posts that allowed me to continue my research programs, focusing on schizophrenia and related challenges confronting the person behind the illness, such as quality of psychiatric care and its evaluation. Broadening the concept of outcomes, this included important functional aspects such as quality of life and subjective tolerability to medication, which became one of our research priorities. Our thirty-year project uncovered the psychoneurobiology of why a number of patients suffering from schizophrenia hated to take their medications, leading to frequent relapse and readmission to hospitals, the well-known revolving door phenomenon. Discovering the connection of the dysphoric dislike of antipsychotics and its origin in the dopamine function of the striatal region of the brain, brought a deeper understanding of the frequent comorbid use and abuse of illicit drugs in schizophrenia, as both phenomena, subjective tolerability to medications and comorbid addictions, share the same dopamine system. This discovery introduced a new way of choosing the right medications for treatment of such disruptive comorbid substance abuse.

After fifty years of academic services and contributions, I feel fortunate and grateful to the many trainees who enrolled in our clinical research programs over the years and to all the colleagues who served and collaborated with me in our research programs. My gratitude also extends to the many patients who inspired us and helped in focusing our research attention on what matters to them.

On the other hand, following and observing psychiatric practices in the past few years from a close, inside perspective, I feel progressively concerned, as do a few other international senior psychiatrists, about the slow pace of progress in psychiatric science and practice. Progress has been discontinuous, with a few peaks frequently separated by long and stagnant periods. Seriously considering and debating all aspects and issues that delay further progress, I cannot change my unfortunate conclusion that current psychiatric practices continue to fail many: patients and their families, their psychiatrists and the society at large. Patients are still struggling with mostly ineffective and risky treatments, whether it be medications or, more frequently, expensive lengthy psychotherapies that can also be of questionable quality and impacts families. Similarly, families are struggling with the burden of care, with its serious emotional, physical and economic impact. Psychiatrists are dissatisfied with the continued erosion of their role and the lack of effectiveness of treatments, as well as several unmet needs both in science and practice. The average psychiatrist feels burdened by a lack of backing by strong science and practicing in an overloaded, underfunded and fragmented service model.

And that is the point where I stopped my discourse that informed readers in my recent book, "The Search For a New Psychiatry", published in 2021. That was also the point where I began searching for new approaches that can truly reform psychiatry and help in securing the future of psychiatry as a scientific medical specialty. Projecting my thoughts forward, I became convinced that the future of psychiatry, to a considerable degree, can benefit from embracing the new and rapidly evolving approaches of "information technologies". This is the crux of the dialogue I am planning to continue with my readers in this book: "Can Artificial Intelligence and Big Data Save the Future of Psychiatry?".

But Then the Covid-19 Pandemic Hit Hard – Necessity Brings Creativity

By late summer of 2018, the research preparation for the 2021 book had been mostly completed. An extensive list of references and reading resources had already been arranged. My thoughts, observations and experiences were more or less grouped into a workable writing plan that would guide me in developing the manuscript, barring any sudden events that could change my thoughts and my plans. In essence, I intended to pursue my usual approach that worked well with previous books I had written, except for one major difference. While previous books were mostly rooted in scientific data, experimentation and research interpretations, the 2021 book was more personally based and followed my biography as the framework for dealing with experiences of science as I perceived and practiced it on three continents, in Cairo, Moscow, briefly back to Cairo and on to Rome and then, ultimately, to Toronto. The biographically and experientially based narrative followed the outline, as described in the previous chapter. With that clear plan, composing the manuscript got started in earnest and with great enthusiasm, encouraged by the clarity of my thoughts concerning what I wanted to share with the readers as the major highlights of the book.

By mid-December 2019, a few news dispatches from China briefly noted the incidence of a mysterious illness in the city of Wuhan, that inflicted serious lung and acute respiratory difficulties. The brief news clip did not catch adequate attention, being a rather minor item in the back pages of newspapers. It was even brushed-off at the highest political level by the then president of the United States, who stated it would be no more than an episode of influenza and by the end of the week would be gone. It wasn't. In a few days the Chinese authorities announced that the virus behind the mysterious lethal and quickly spreading illness was identified as a member of a wide class of viruses known as corona virus. It was the same class of virus that was behind several epidemics, with the most recent in memory being MERS (Middle East Respiratory Syndrome) and SARS (Severe Acute Respiratory Syndrome), both of which were well-known after they invaded several countries including North America not that long ago. Both pandemics proved to be lethal and highly contagious.

That was the point when, coupled with the reported high mortality rate caused by the new Covid-19 infection, the world took notice and was unprepared to deal with it, lacking an adequate means or vaccine to handle it. By early 2020, the Covid-19 virus had become widespread. Though China had invoked isolation, quarantine and lock-down measures, the Covid-19 virus, as happened in previous pandemics, seemed not to recognize boundaries or respect borders. Panic and anxiety prevailed, followed by more strict measures and prolonged periods of lock-down. Among a clear disarray at all government levels, the crisis became complicated by suspicion and a multitude of conspiracy theories. Life, business and social activities slowed down to a virtual halt.

It was at that point that I recognized I had plenty of free time, as a result of the long lock-downs. Though my psychiatric consultations managed to continue by phone, to the relief of many patients, I still felt that I had a good deal of time to spare. Initially, I assumed the newly found free time would accelerate the development of the manuscript, to the point that I thought the publication date could be advanced. However, on the contrary, having enforced free time and the loss of my daily routine patterns, particularly social activities, dampened and slowed the creative moment rather than enhancing it. Though a low degree of tension and anxiety can prove helpful in maintaining the creative process, at least in my case, the fear, anxiety and near panic all around me became a distraction.

The chaos and disarray continued through the various strata of society. Medical issues such as the lethal and rapidly spreading Covid-19 pandemic and a desperate search for the best way to contain it, became a highly contested political issue that confused and further misled the public. Overall, the alarm, fear and anxiety continued, becoming routine and aggravated by the standstill of economic and social activities. Time quickly became a waiting game for any good news regarding the development of vaccines or more effective medications and, ultimately, a better control of the epidemic. Such was the case until late 2020, when encouraging news arrived about the successful results of a clinical trial of an effective vaccine using a new technique based on mRNA research, which will be discussed in the next chapter. It was a glimmer of hope and optimism, on the background of continuing disarray and desperation.

With the optimistic announcement of the early results of the new vaccine in clinical trials, contrasted with the mismanagement of the pandemic and the many holes and gaps in the public health system revealed to the public for the first time, there was an important and almost miraculous scientific story occurring in parallel time and hidden in the many labs around the world that were quietly collaborating and working on the production of the new Covid-19 vaccine. By the end of 2020 and early 2021, several new vaccines were available for use, to the relief and comfort of the worried population. Developing an effective vaccine in less than a year, instead of the traditional several years, was received as short of a miraculous scientific story. It was built on major scientific advances in several fields, such as molecular genetics, microbiology, virology and medical technologies, all packed and facilitated by a new approach that utilized the benefits from the evolving information technologies of artificial intelligence and big data analytics. It was a new era of scientific progress and how major scientific challenges can be handled by international collaborative consortia, sharing information, expertise and resources. This is the surprising reason for me to include such a fascinating story about the development of a vaccine in a book related to the future of psychiatry.

Meanwhile, my book titled "The Search For a New Psychiatry – On Becoming a Psychiatrist and Clinical Neuroscientist and Other Fragments of Memory" was published in July 2021, by the highly expert iUniverse publishing company in Indiana, USA. The book, to my great satisfaction, was well received and so far has managed to create discussion, which certainly was my objective. In August 2021, the book managed to reach the Amazon best sellers list for new releases in the category of Medical Biography. Most recently, the book and myself were honoured in a gracious review by Professor Santosh

Chaturvedi in Springer's Journal of Psychosocial Rehabilitation and Mental Health. Similarly, another review of the book was posted by the electronic site of the International Network for the History of Neuropsychopharmacology, which is based in Sweden.

Altogether, preparing a manuscript and getting it rapidly published during the time of the pandemic proved to be a challenge, but also a very interesting experience. The successful story about how the Covid-19 vaccine was designed and produced has left me with a good deal of reflection on such a process and whether it represents how science and its applications are going to be dealt with in the future, based on the accumulated strong basic sciences and facilitated by the use of new information technological advances.

The Rapidly Evolving Information Technology (IT)

Information technology or IT, as it is widely referred to, is the study and application of computers and telecommunications to store, retrieve and transmit data. It involves techniques for the fast processing of information and the use of elaborate mathematical and statistical models for decision-making. It can also involve the simulation of higher-level thinking, through the process of computer programming. The use of information technology permeates many aspects of our daily life, including education, healthcare, transportation, economics and many other fields. Examples include tasks and services attained through our smart phones, Zoom video meetings, paying for our e-bills and glancing through Netflix, all of which use AI. It is hard these days to find an aspect of our current life that does not include one form or another of the rapidly evolving information technology. For the purpose of focusing its potential applications in psychiatry and its relevance in the future, in the next several chapters I will concentrate on three major applications: Artificial intelligence (AI), big data sets (BD) and analytics.

The Science and Technology Behind the Development of the New mRNA Covid 19 Vaccine – Why it is Relevant to Psychiatry

The story of the development of the first vaccine based on the use of mRNA technology is a very intriguing and rather convoluted story that includes all of the complications involved in a major scientific discovery; fierce rivalry among scientists, the clash between science and commercialism, patents, intellectual property rights, acrimony and endless litigation. One of the reasons for such a state is the incremental scientific discoveries and research stretching over decades, which usually includes a number of scientists, entrepreneurs, fund raisers and investors, many of whom are recognized, while others are almost forgotten.

In this brief introduction regarding the history of the amazing and promising discovery of the Covid-19 vaccine, I'd like to clarify a few terms, such as DNA, RNA and mRNA, which will be mentioned frequently in this text and are at the core of this fascinating story.

What is DNA?

DNA, or deoxyribonucleic acid, is the unit that carries heredity in humans and is located mostly in the cell nucleus, however, a small amount can also be found in cell mitochondria. Since DNA cannot leave the cell nucleus to carry instructions needed for development, growth and reproduction, the DNA sequences have to be converted into messages known as RNA, that can leave the nucleus to instruct the machinery capable of producing proteins, which are the complex molecules that do most of the work in the human body. DNA are packaged tightly in a chromosome and each DNA sequence that contains instructions to make a protein is known as a gene. The complete set of nuclear DNA is referred to as the genome, which contains about three billion bases and about 20,000 genes on 23 pairs of chromosomes. This amazing information first became available through the early discoveries of the Swiss scientist Friedrich Miescher in 1869, who isolated DNA from cell nuclei. This early starting point in the field of genetics was inspired by the observations made a few years earlier by the botanist and scientist Gregor Mendel in 1865, who noted that heredity in peas could be transmitted in discrete units.

From Peas to Genome

Such early breakthroughs by Miescher and Mendel slowly and incrementally paved the way to major modern developments decades later. In 1953, the double helix structure of DNA was discovered by James Watson, Francis Crick and their collaborators Maurice Wilkins and Rosalind Franklin. By the year 2003, the completion of the Human Genome Project, to an exceptional accuracy, had left scientists with a massive amount of scientific information that would keep them busy for decades, in their quest for a better understanding of human diseases and the prospect of the development of better, more effective and safer medications. Such extraordinary genomic information has also provided the first real opportunity for the development of personalized medicine and the beginning of precision medicine in psychiatry, as will be discussed in a later chapter.

What is RNA, mRNA?

RNA, or ribonucleic acid, is the molecule that can leave the nucleus of the cell to carry genetic instructions from the DNA to the protein-making machinery in the ribosomes in cytoplasm. It also stores genetic information and it has been suggested by some scientists to have a role in the beginning of the process of life itself. Basically, the RNA are the ones to connect the DNA to the protein factories in the cells and to regulate genes. The designation of mRNA refers to its function as a messenger.

The interesting story behind the discovery of RNA goes back to 1961, when two French scientists, Jacque Monod and Francois Jacob, suggested that the existence of a molecule such as mRNA was the transporter of genetic information from the DNA to the protein "factories" in the ribosomes in the cytoplasm. This conclusion was based on their observation that the DNA information could not leave the cell nucleus to impact the protein machines in the cytoplasm of cells. It is interesting that the whole science of the RNA story was started by these two French scientists, but their role is rarely recognized. This is not a unique story, as the fierce science competition for who was first to make a discovery or who has contributed more is a well-known science event, particularly when it comes to patents, prestigious awards and lucrative royalties.

The process of the RNA discovery was slow and incremental, and took decades to advance after the discovery of DNA in 1869. Yet, in its recent modern history, RNA captured a good deal of scientific interest, although it had no clinical medical application established other than some limited trials in the field of oncology, until the recent breakthrough in the development of the Covid-19 vaccine. The major barrier and challenge for its medical use was the need to modify the mRNA molecule to avoid being destroyed by the body's immune system, as it could potentially create some serious immune reactions.

One of the names that succeeded in modifying the mRNA molecule was the Hungarian-born scientist Katalin Kariko, who developed a major research interest in the mRNA system. She had incredible determination and perseverance, but somewhat typical of such stories, she lacked research funding and adequate recognition in her native country of Hungary, and therefore moved to the USA for more secure funding and the continuation of her mRNA research. In 1997 she teamed up with a colleague, Drew Weissman, who was studying dendritic cells. Their collaboration eventually provided a breakthrough in 2005, of modifying the mRNA molecule to be developed into therapy in human beings. In 2008, they extended an invitation of collaboration to include another Harvard scientist, Derrick Rossi, who was trying to use mRNA to make stem cells, but he had been confronted with the same difficulty Dr. Kariko had initially experienced before she modified the mRNA molecule.

Professor Rossi, in need of more funding to pursue his project, turned to many major investors and, as a result, the development of the new company "Moderna" was established to support his work. At that point, the major contributions by Kariko and Weissman began to pay off in establishing the field of mRNA modification and positioning it to what may certainly become the future of vaccine development and other new medical therapies, particularly in areas such as oncology and cardiovascular conditions. The moral in such a somewhat convoluted story, and by including it in a book about the future of psychiatry, is basically related to its applicability in the development of medical research of the future. Obviously, the story is more complex and involves more than a few major contributors and a lot of twists, challenges, disagreements and much more than what is included in this brief review. The lessons gained can be simply summarized into a few important points:

- Challenging medical research questions, hopefully including psychiatric unresolved issues such as schizophrenia and bipolar disorder, can be handled much better by a national and international consortia that pools expertise, information and funding
- Central to such a success, the value of big data sets in generating patterns and information cannot be over emphasized. This is where new information technology, such as artificial intelligence and big data analytics, can play a major role
- As happened in the expedient case of the Covid-19 vaccine development, governmental agencies need to play a major role in facilitating the process of transfer and security of

data and information by revising rules and establishing new frameworks for sharing data

- Obviously, the current success of mRNA research owes it to accumulated and ongoing basic strong research and knowledge in the fields of genetics, microbiology, virology, medical and information technologies, and several others. Progress and advances do not happen in mid-air, but are based on the accumulated development of strong basic sciences and research methodologies that need to be continually updated and enhanced.

Finally, the question that urgently poses itself is whether the successful outcome of the development of mRNA vaccines can be replicated in other fields? More specifically, can it be replicated to serve the future of psychiatry?

Artificial Intelligence (AI)

a) A Brief Historical Account

Artificial intelligence, as defined by the Oxford dictionary, is an approach based on theory and development of powerful computer systems capable of performing various tasks that normally require human intelligence. It is a brand of the fast and ever expanding field of computer sciences in collaboration with advanced engineering, and with contributions from multiple other fields such as psychology, neurobiology, neurosciences and philosophy.

Though the year 1950 is credited as the beginning of the modern concept of artificial intelligence, its history goes back to ancient Egyptians, Chinese, Greek and Roman times. Greco-Roman mythology included allusions to mechanical devices or contraptions to help the gods in carrying out heavy tasks. During the first century, Heron of Alexandria created what was called mechanical men and automatons. By the year AD 800, the book of Geber was published by the Persian scientist and Arabian alchemist Jabir ibn Hayyan and included the theory of "takwin", the artificial creation of life in the laboratory, including humans. In 1580, the Rabbi Judah Loew ben Bezalal invented the "golem" in Prague, a clay man brought to life. It seems that such concepts were explored to reflect the deep wish and urge for humans to reproduce copies of themselves. The fascination with concepts related to what we now call "artificial intelligence" proceeded over centuries in different forms or embedded in fantasy and often included in weird and scary novels, unencumbered by science and only limited by the fantastic imagination of its authors.

In 1837, a mathematician named Charles Babbage developed what was considered to be the first programmable machine, the "analytic engine". The machine did not work well, and in an attempt to help her friend with his invention, Ada Byron, also known as Countess Lovelace and the daughter of the great English poet Lord Byron, decided to write a series of extensive programs for the analytic machine. Eventually Countess Lovelace teamed up with Babbage to develop a rapid chess machine to help fund a large, new building to house her programs and machines. Work on the analytic engine did not succeed, but the Countess has been credited with the development of the field of software programming. In the end, she summed up her disappointment by stating that the analytic machine had no pretensions whatsoever to originate anything and that other machines like it can do only what we tell them to do. However, she left open the question of whether such machines are able to think and to await a time when one would be built and tested.

Even with the failure of the analytic engine project, efforts to develop an intelligent machine continued. By 1890, the first machine to record and store information with punch cards was developed by Herman Hollerith, which eventually was used in conducting the US census process. Several years later, this new development grew extensively to eventually become the core of the well known IBM

Corporation. The establishment of IBM seemed to add more fantasies and fascination with robots and intelligent machines. Publication of several fantasy tales and books continued unabated, contributing to the development of the ever expanding field of science fiction.

In 1919, the well known Czech writer Karel Capek published his fantastic science fiction and futuristic play "Rossum's Universal Robots". The play dealt with factory made artificial people, and for the first time the word "robot" was introduced, as a derivative of the Slavic word "rabota", meaning work. Karel Capek is also well known for a series of excellent books that includes his satire "The War With the Salamanders". It was written in 1936, as a highly political satire imagining and predicting what actually occurred in Nazi Germany shortly afterwards, and how appeasing evil and undemocratic powers can end in a catastrophe. Several similar books followed, including the Wizard of Oz and its character of the Tin Man. The broad expansion of the science fiction genre brought more familiarity with the concept of artificial intelligence and heightened society's expectations for such challenging scientific developments. Altogether, by the 19th century, not only was society familiar with the "robot world" through fantasy books, but was also prepared to watch its real materialization.

The young mathematician Alan Turing designed a prototype of the "Turing Machine" in 1937, a device used for the computing of numbers, which apparently was initially met with derision and taken only half-seriously. Yet, his engrossing fascination and hobby continued and peaked in 1950 by introducing his "Turing Test", as a measure of machine intelligence. His seminal paper "Computing Machinery and Intelligence", proved to be the opening shot for the development of the modern era of computers and intelligence. Another big name of that era was John von Neumann, the Hungarian/ American mathematician whose early work paved the way for the development of powerful computers and computer science. As well, Conrad Zuse, was a young German technologist who built a machine similar to Turing's in his parent's living room, which he introduced in 1943. He followed this in 1945, by developing a programming language for solving difficult mathematical problems and for use in programming artificial intelligence challenges. With his important inventions, Conrad Zuse was almost a decade away from the later explosion of interest in the subject of intelligent machines and artificial intelligence.

It was also a time of a significant shift from the dominant physics notion of energy to a new paradigm of cybernetics of information technology that described biological and psychological phenomena in clear mathematical terms. As a result of such a convergence and the noticeable scientific interest in the subject of AI, a young mathematics professor, John McCarthy, at Dartmouth College in Hanover, New Hampshire, decided to organize a meeting inclusive of only ten persons active in the field of AI. The purpose was to discuss and share their work experiences. In the end, far more than ten persons attended the meeting that was held at Dartmouth College in 1956, and funded by major foundations such as the Rockefeller and Rand Foundations. The meeting was open and informal, allowing other scientists to drop in and out and share their work. Among the important presentations was one about a program called the "Logic Theorist", which was designed to mimic the problem-solving skills of human beings. Since then, it has been considered the first presentation of an artificial intelligence program. Certainly, the Dartmouth Summer Project meeting in 1956 is where the term "artificial intelligence" was coined. Though the meeting in 1956 ended short of its ambitious objective to produce and agree on standards and methods to guide the evolving field, by all accounts the Dartmouth meeting served as a catalyst and guided the development of the field of AI research for the next two decades. The meeting at Dartmouth College in Hanover, New Hampshire in 1956 is certainly credited as a major milestone and turning point in the history of AI research and its application.

During the twenty years that followed, computer technology has vastly improved in speed and capacity, as well as becoming less expensive. Machine learning algorithms equally improved and the use of the right algorithm for a specific problem has also improved. More research funding became available from the private sector and from government agencies, particularly from the US Defence Department and, specifically, from the Defence Advanced Research Projects Agency known as DARPA. It certainly was an optimistic and productive era in the field of AI. However, certain obstacles continued to limit the field, such as a lack of computer power and the capacity to store enormous data files. By 1980, the situation was improved by the availability of more funding and an expansion of algorithms. By 1990, computers were more powerful and more innovative. It was during the decade of 1990-2000 when major public events boosted the interest and progress of the AI field. In 1997, the world chess champion grand master Gary Kasparov was defeated by IBM's "Deep Blue" chess playing computer. At the same time, speech recognition software developed by Dragon Systems was introduced on "Windows", which also led to language interpretation capabilities. All that made computers powerful and able to do many tasks. Even in the field of emotions, a robot named Kismet could recognize and display very simple emotions, reflected in facial expressions, as an early phase in the future important development in emotion and facial recognition.

At present, we are living in an exceptional time for supercomputers and expanding artificial intelligence capabilities that have found their way into many aspects of our daily life, from paying our e-bills to analyzing huge data sets that search for patterns and trends to enhance predictive capabilities. AI approaches have already permeated through business, education and in medicine, from neuroimaging to scheduling and follow-up appointments. From maps and navigation to driver-less vehicles and into other vast ranges of "assistant" services such as those offered by Google, which I am using in the preparation of this manuscript. Other assistant services have also been introduced, like "Siri" and "Alexa".

Applications in healthcare have improved quality, access, organization and management of healthcare services. It also provides the potential for scientific breakthroughs, such as in the miraculous rapid introduction of mRNA-based modern Covid-19 vaccines. It certainly can get us closer to precision medicine and precision psychiatry, tailoring the treatment to the individual, with the right dose at the right time. At present, a large chunk of medical care has moved to becoming almost fully digital, which facilitates the process of care and would greatly enhance the next move to information technologies, as represented by AI and big data technologies.

Though more details will be included in the next few chapters, regarding the benefits, possible risks and limitations of such evolving technologies and, with all of the many pluses of these technological advances already in use, I hasten to pose the question of why there is a noticeably low level of interest in the psychiatric field and among psychiatrists?

Artificial Intelligence (AI): Levels, Benefits and Risks

• **Levels and Categorization of Artificial Intelligence**

The various types of artificial intelligence are based on the degree to which AI systems can closely replicate human capabilities. Several types of AI do exist, including up to seven categories, with a good deal of overlapping among them. However, in terms of use, the Four Categories and Three Categories models are the ones more frequently in use.

○ **The Four Category AI Model**

• **Reactive AI**

It has no memory, only responds to tasks. Have limited capabilities and have no ability to learn.

• **Limited Memory AI**

Uses memory to learn and improve its responses and make decisions. All current AI systems in use are of this type. They are trained by the large volume of data that inform models for solving problems. This model includes deep learning capabilities, virtual assistance, chat bots and several other capabilities.

• **Theory of Mind AI**

This is the next level of systems that are not available yet, but do exist as an experimental model and is on the category of "work in progress". Theory of Mind is a psychological concept meaning the capacity to understand other people's emotions, feelings, their thought processes and their minds as unique individual entities. It functions in a somewhat similar manner to the common parlance phrase "reading your mind". Such a level of AI intelligence requires extensive development, not only in the field of AI, but also in several other related fields. It is a major challenge, as such AI machines have to be able to perceive an individual human beings' mind, which can be affected by many other factors.

• **Self-Aware AI**

This AI type has human-like intelligence and self-awareness. In other words, such systems are at par with humans or even better in certain situations. Such a level has not yet been achieved. It is still a hypothetical construct that may take a long time to become real, or it may not happen at all. This type of AI not only can evoke emotions through interactions, but also has its own emotions and beliefs. This is the type which is most dreaded and feared, as it can potentially lead to crises and disasters as a result of being self-aware and having its own thoughts. In a sense, they can potentially develop schemes and plots that can endanger humanity. This type is a major challenge that the society in general has to anticipate and with it effectively plan in advance before it is created. Though that may take a long time and is still far away, it will be an ominous and dangerous development when it happens.

◦ **The Three Category AI Model**

In practice, the three categories model is the one most used, as it is much simpler.

• **Artificial Narrow Intelligence (ANI)**

This type includes all existing AI machines that can perform autonomously specific tasks using human-like capabilities. They cannot do anything beyond what they are programmed to do and that is the reason for defining them as having a narrow range. The ANI type corresponds to the *reactive* and *limited* memory types in the Four Categories model.

• **Artificial General Intelligence (AGI)**

This type is expected to be at par with human capabilities to learn, understand and function like human beings.

• **Artificial Super Intelligence (ASI)**

If such a type could exist in the far away future, it would be the ultimate in AI research and development. It can probably exceed human intelligence and that will be the danger, as described in the Four Categories model.

• Benefits: What AI Can Provide

AI can provide a broad array of programmable functions that include planning, learning, reasoning, problem-solving and making decisions. AI systems are powered by algorithms that employ deep learning (the ability of multiple layers of neurons to extract more information). Machine learning algorithms, in turn, feed computers data to AI systems using statistical techniques to enable AI systems to learn. In recent years, AI systems have been getting progressively better at tasks without having to be specifically programmed.

The ability of machines with multiple layers of neurons, as like the real brain, has proven to be more capable of extracting much higher levels of features from the raw input. It has significantly improved the performance in several important subprograms, such as computer vision, voice recognition and image classification, among many other important fields. In general, AI can provide a long list of benefits:

- Increase work efficiencies and saving time and labour in training.
- Introduce high levels of accuracy and reduce errors.
- Reduce costs through automation.
- Improve a large number of processes contributing to modern ways of life, such as searching the internet, e-banking, smartphones, analysis of big data sets and several other assisting services, like the editorial assistance that I am using right now in composing this chapter.

- **AI Risks and Harms**

1. Joblessness, particularly in repetitive jobs, though a number of experts believe that jobs may evolve rather than be totally lost.

2. Threat to humanity, in the case of AI supercomputers having been created with the potential of their operations going rogue by creating plots, catastrophes and dangerous chaotic states, as described above. A number of imminent scientists, such as the late Stephen Hawking, who is on record as stating that the development of AI super computers could spell the end of the human race. Even big investors in AI research and development, such as the entrepreneur Elon Musk, declared that AI poses the biggest existential threat if developed carelessly.

3. Sustainability may become a major threat, as a result of the overproduction of computer chips that can exhaust natural resources of rare metals, including silicone, lithium and several others. As noted recently, with the production of chips disrupted as a result of the Covid-19 pandemic and the state of emergency related to the Russian invasion of Ukraine, a noticeable supply impact has followed, particularly in car manufacturing and other businesses.

- **AI Ethical and Legal Risks**

  ◦ Issues about sources of data and possible violations of personal privacy
  ◦ Black box algorithms that can lead to serious issues about transparency
  ◦ Secrecy and lack of appropriate traceability
  ◦ Lack of legal accountability
  ◦ Potential development of lethal autonomous weapon systems

- ## **Potential and Unintentional Racial Bias**

Unexplained and potentially unethical, a recent observation was noted while testing AI-based driverless cars, regarding the ability of such vehicles to detect objects or pedestrians with various skin colours. Regardless of several modifications to the model used, it consistently emerged that it was much harder for such models to see dark-skinned persons walking around. If not corrected, such a major flaw can lead to injuries sustained by people with dark skin. Similarly, such a flaw can impair facial recognition of dark-skinned people. It can also have medical implications in the dermatological diagnosis of dark moles. It is a major ethical and medical challenge that requires an appropriate resolution. Recently, the European community, China, US and several other countries, as well as the Organization for Economic Cooperation and Development, has instituted bodies for strategic development and ethical advocacy of AI technology. More recently, in Canada the government introduced to parliament the Artificial Intelligence and Data Act (AIDA). Presumably, such an act is to constrain development within ethical boundaries and not to let AI developers run amok.

- ## **Potential for Plagiarism and Confabulation**

The very recent introduction of "ChatGPT" by OpenAI, shortly followed by Google's "Bard", has introduced major language processing models that are pre-trained with a massive amount of data and are capable of generating human-like texts. Within a very short time, such models have gained immense popularity because of their applicability in business, medicine and several other important and practical fields. On the other hand, as a result of their extensive use, certain serious limitations have been noted, such as the potential for plagiarism, which has raised serious concerns about their misuse in colleges and academic circles.

Similarly, another noted issue is an uncertainty with the accuracy of their information. Though they are widely recognized as mostly accurate, there are occasional concerns with their veracity, which can be difficult to identify and can present as a type of "confabulation". This brings to my recollection an old and serious medical and neuropsychiatric memory problem known as Korsakoff psychosis, which has a distinct confabulatory presentation as one of its clinical features. It is a degeneration of the brain as a consequence of excessive and long-term alcohol abuse, although its pathophysiology continues to be unclear. One of the most recent theories noted is that such confabulation is not a deliberate lie, but is based on true information brought back from memory stores and generally placed in the wrong sequence. Not to say that wrong sequencing is one of the origins of confabulatory incidents with ChatGPT and Bard, but it is certainly worth exploring (a very recent reference: King MR, ChatGPT. A Conversation on Artificial Intelligence, Chatbots and Plagiarism in Higher Education, Cel Mol Bioengineering 2023, 16:1-2)

- **Application of AI Technology in Medicine**

Several AI approaches have already been in use in medicine and medical care and seem to have potentially revolutionized healthcare. They have provided new capabilities in diagnostic challenges, as in the most recent example that was detailed before: screening for Covid-19 viral infections. The ability to screen data more accurately and in-depth can detect disease biomarkers that would not be detected with other traditional searches. The diagnostic process can become more predictable and precise, which is a major help in treatments and management of diseases. Better diagnostics and management can certainly lead to better outcomes and more containment of the spiralling costs of healthcare.

At the present time, AI and big data analytics have already transformed practices in some medical specialties, such as medical imaging, cardiovascular, ophthalmology and potentially a few others. Enabling the use of massive information generated by the human genome project can enhance predictive strategies and gets us closer to precise medicine by tailoring the treatment to the individual patient, as will be discussed in a later chapter on the recent and imminent advances in the field of pharmacogenomics.

AI can play a role in all stages of developing new medications, which is a lengthy and complex process. It can cut down on time and cost in the early phase of searching for useful molecules for development, among thousands of possible molecules. It can also impact on reforming and improving clinical trials phases two and three, as well as facilitate post-marketing surveillance. AI can help the process of healthcare administration, in terms of appointments and follow-up, as well as management of extensive clinical care information and medical records, making it organized, integrated and seamless. AI may eventually fulfill the futuristic prediction of Professor Michael Snyder, regarding the new role of future physicians by accessing the genomic information of a patient at the press of a button, detecting their vulnerabilities and tailoring their treatment, as described in a later chapter.

• **Artificial Intelligence in Psychiatry**

AI has comparatively made significant inroads in medicine and healthcare in recent years, but in psychiatry it is still in its very early infancy. Even the small amount that so far has been done in psychiatry seems to be more of an individual or specific institutional effort and not yet as part of a wider national effort, as evidenced by the sparse AI publications in major mainstream psychiatric journals and websites. There is hesitancy and mixed views among psychiatrists about the applicability of AI research in psychiatry, which will be reviewed and discussed in a later chapter.

In reality, psychiatry as a medical discipline is one of the most suited to benefit from AI technology, both in science and its application in psychiatric care organizations. The ongoing etiological challenges in understanding the origins of major psychiatric illness and its relationship to specific brain functions continues to be an elusive mystery. Psychiatric treatments need overhauling and much needed improvement. Developing diagnostic approaches and a more precise description of symptoms, in addition to a much better diagnostic classification system, can make psychiatric management more organized and predictable. It certainly can make choosing psychiatry as a career choice more attractive to bright and interested medical trainees. Above all, it can significantly improve psychiatric treatments for the benefit of psychiatric patients in their long term painful sufferings.

The Current State of Artificial Intelligence in Medicine and Psychiatry, and the Reasons for Low Interest Among Psychiatrists

AI in Medicine

Over the recent few decades there have been noticeable refinements and a rapid expansion of several aspects of information technologies, including artificial intelligence and big data analytics, that allow for its use in several medical specialties such as radiology, oncology, ophthalmology and dermatology, as well as evolving in others, such as cardiology. Several studies have already documented the benefits of AI in medical imaging, even proving its superiority in certain medical conditions. In ophthalmology, there have been reports about the ability of AI to diagnose rare retinal diseases that cannot be spotted by traditional human approaches. There is already a good body of knowledge regarding the application of AI and big data analysis in medicine, particularly in the understanding of disease process and its progression. It can enable disease detection in the early phase or reveal rare forms of a disease, which can improve outcomes. AI is already on its way of providing a more precise tailoring of medications to the individual patients, getting us closer to precision medicine.

Outside of medicine, AI technology has managed to occupy a sizable space in our routine daily activities, from e-banking, smart phones and searching the internet, to flipping through Netflix for program choices, and so many other applications. These many applications proceed with the full recognition of IT limitations, possible risks and the need for appropriate ethical oversight. At the same time, there is a recognition that AI and information technology are neither a panacea nor a magic bullet for all of our challenges. AI is not a replacement for humans, but a vehicle and a method among other approaches, that enables us to exercise our medical role more precisely and efficiently.

AI in Psychiatry and the Reasons for Low Interest Among Psychiatrists

Reviewing the state and application of AI approaches in psychiatry, it is clear that it is in its early infancy, gauging by the volume and breadth of AI-related published reports. The impression one gets is that most published reports are basically pockets of individual or institutional efforts, and do not represent a formal or systematic professional framework that embraces this new technology nor systematically attempts to reap its benefits. Worse, a few recent surveys among psychiatrists clearly have demonstrated a major division in the pros and cons of AI technology, with generally low interest, which is also consistent with my own observations.

A recent global study conducted by Professor Murali Doraiswamy and his colleagues from Duke University in the US, which also included 791 practising psychiatrists in twenty-two countries across Europe, the Americas and Asia Pacific, demonstrated a clear split and differences of opinion among the respondents, related to their thinking about AI technology for the future of psychiatry. The study included questions that asked whether AI technology can replace key tasks carried out in general psychiatric practices. The results, published in 2019, showed that among the respondents only 3.8% felt that AI future technology would make their jobs obsolete. Roughly one in two respondents agreed that AI could impact their role as psychiatrists, but that was related to only two tasks, the excessive burden of documentation and updating medical records and, overall, the task of providing a synthesis of the collected information. The respondents did not think AI was capable of other tasks such as improving diagnosis or adding precision to treatments. One of the interesting findings of the survey was that female participating psychiatrists and US-based psychiatrists, in general, were uncertain about whether the benefits of AI technology would outweigh the risks. Though the study was limited by the range of the questions included, and with consideration of the issue of whether the global sample truly represented the broader constituency of psychiatrists, the survey provided compelling insights about the fears, concerns and a possible lack of knowledge among psychiatrists. In contrast, other surveys among radiologists, ophthalmologists, medical internists and neurologists have provided a more positive attitude towards the future of AI and information technologies in general, related to their respective areas of practice. Though young radiologists in training felt that AI may replace some jobs, the majority of respondents felt the acquired precision is an important and welcomed practice.

Back to the somewhat disappointing results of the survey in psychiatry, for me it has not been a surprise. Anytime issues related to new technology, specifically AI technology, was mentioned to colleagues, the immediate concern of losing the empathic approach inherent in the practice of psychiatry was quickly raised, with no consideration that any clarification provided by AI is an enabler, rather than an alternative to the human psychiatrist. Behind the computer programs and development of computational algorithms there is always a human-being, but in the end, that discussion does not change many minds. With very few exceptions, the discussion inevitably ends up as a battle between humans versus machines. Obviously, the issue of losing empathy is frequently a red herring that betrays a lack of knowledge and a misinterpretation. Though more concerns have been noted among psychiatrists who only provide psychotherapy, in recent years there have been more voices of expert psychotherapists who have expressed an optimistic view of the new information technologies and its potential role in improving accessibility and the development of more effective models of therapy.

The reality is that information technologies are not going away any time soon. They are here to stay. Concern regarding the potential divestment of medical care to private corporations and insurance companies is real and is already shaping the rules that guide practice, but without a major input from practising psychiatrists or physicians in its development. To mitigate such a negative impact, there is an urgent need for psychiatrists and physicians in general, to team up with the private sector and third parties in developing the appropriate rules that guide and regulate practices in the era of the wide use of information technologies.

One of the major gaps in psychiatry has been the failure of psychiatric training curricula to prepare psychiatrists for future challenges. To do so, those in charge of the development of such a curricula must have eyes wide open and a creative imagination regarding future developments. Many training curricula go stale quickly, packed with the foundational past, but missing where the field is going or ought to be heading. The historical split of psychiatry and neurology has contributed to some erosion of the basic science base behind brain functioning, with less interest and curiosity about technological advances that can broaden our understanding of basic brain functions.

Another limiting factor for acquiring knowledge about advances in information technologies and its role in medicine, has been the paucity of published research reports on the subject in mainstream psychiatric journals, which are more accessible to the average psychiatrist. Though the majority of AI and big data research reports have been more often published in specialized journal or websites, recently, few mainstream psychiatric journals, such as JAMA and The Lancet, have been devoting more space for such contributions. It is encouraging to note that the major journal Neuropsychopharmacology, has recently devoted the first issue of 2021 to include contributions about AI, big data, neuroimaging and other related topics, including critical analysis and helpful future trends.

Another major factor that contributes to a lack of enthusiasm and knowledge about the new field of information technologies has been the issues of funding, a lack of recognition as a major trend in medicine and the absence of a national or professional formal framework that guides and supports the development of this evolving field. AI and big data technologies are already in use and are rapidly spreading, but before researching the basics of such technologies as applied to medicine, there needs to be professional and scientific bodies that guide the field, help and support standards and encourage the development of consortia that pool expertise and resources. There are many parties, besides scientists and technical experts, who need to be brought into the discussion of this evolving field. Governments at all levels need to also be engaged, as their role in the transfer and security of data is important.

Another important partner in such discussions is regulatory and academic professional colleges. It is most encouraging to note the recent endorsement of the Royal College of Physicians and Surgeons of Canada for the integration of digital and information technologies, such as AI and big data analytics, in clinical practice and including it in training curricula. It is a bold and enlightened decision that confirms the recent progressive agenda of the College being ahead of many other colleges in accurately reading and interpreting the future of medicine. I am lauding this important decision, in contrast to thirty or forty years ago when the College was mostly conservative and more concerned with preserving the status quo. I can recall my, and many others', disappointment at the time the College was designing a program for the maintenance of competence, then opting for a weak and ineffective program that was based on reading a journal or attending a conference, tools that would not introduce much improvement in quality of care. Obviously, and thanks to the recent generations that have joined the leadership of the College, attitudes have changed and become progressive, allowing for, but also challenging, decisions such as those of medical informatics to be made.

A Brief Account of the Royal College of Physicians & Surgeons of Canada re: AI and Emerging Digital Technologies

In 2018, the Royal College of Physicians and Surgeons of Canada (RCPSC) council established a task force on artificial intelligence and emerging digital technologies. The objectives of the task force has been to conduct research into current and future states of such technologies and to provide recommendations of how to meet the challenges and opportunities.

The task force, chaired by Professor Richard Reznik, the Dean of Ontario Northern Medical School, included expert members representing the College "Fellows" and clinical and technical experts in the field, conducted a wide consultative process that included a survey among members of the College. Briefly, as a result, the recommendations approved recently by RCPSC council are as follows:

- Digital health literacy competencies be integrated into CanMED's framework.
- Include a new discipline in the area of clinical informatics.

- Enhance AI in team science. The Royal College should play an active role in supporting fellows and resident affiliates to co-develop, refine, validate and spread AI-enabled technologies.
- AI is a potential democratizer of healthcare by including the patient's perspective in all facets of AI-related decision making, to ensure that multiple diverse perspectives are represented.
- Collaborate with partner organizations to develop, tailor, create and distribute educational offerings related to privacy and other ethical and legal concerns arising from adopting AI into healthcare systems.
- Promote, enable, extend scholarships, education and other forms of support to physicians, that increases knowledge of the social justice implications of AI-based technologies.
- Develop an ongoing monitoring and development strategy to address the need for further recommendations in the field of AI and emerging digital technologies.

Indeed, a bold and most informative document, it is a major step forward. Hopefully, it encourages other colleges and regulatory bodies to do the same. It is clear that the College's decision puts the ball squarely in the medical specialties court, including that of psychiatry. It is to be seen how various medical specialties, including psychiatry, would implement it. My hope is that the next generation of young psychiatrists becomes familiar with technological advances in the field of medical informatics in quality of care, as previously noted in our 1980 book, "Evaluation of Quality of Care in Psychiatry". I also hope that medical informatics becomes formally recognized by medical teams, who receive specialty training and funding, than opting for a weak and ineffective program that was mostly based on reading a journal or casually attending a conference, tools that would not introduce by themselves alone a significant improvement of quality of care, as we clearly documented in our 1980 book: "Evaluation of Quality of Care in Psychiatry".

Artificial Intelligence and Predictive Strategies in Psychiatry

a) Predictive Strategies – A Brief Historical Note

Predicting what the future holds is as old as the history of human beings. Survival imperatives, such as predicting seasons for crop cultivation and weather forecasting for navigation, required the development of predictive strategies. A good example that took place over a thousand years ago, in A.D. 1088, the scientist Abu Ishaq Ibrahim al-Zarqali published his compilations of astronomical data in Toledo, Spain, predicting and documenting the position of the sun, moon and other planets for the following four years. Predictions were and still are important for timing religious and traditional rituals that are tied to the moon. A somewhat humorous and historical anecdote from the middle ages involves the powerful church authorities commissioning astronomers to measure distances between planets, for the purpose of better predicting how many believers it could accommodate. The periodical book "Almanac", an ancient manual for weather predictions to help farmers, has continued to be published since the year 1793. Recently, during the Covid-19 pandemic and ensuing restrictions, several mainstream newspapers continued to publish the daily horoscopes, in spite of attempting to reduce the number of printed pages.

In medicine, prediction of the course of illnesses and treatment outcomes have also gone through a long and often uncertain process, which was mostly no more than clever guessing enhanced by various clinical experiences. Most of the time, predictions boiled down to one simple and well proven formula, which is: those patients who improved in the past were likely to improve in the future. A simple notion that most likely contributed to successful careers for many highly prized and famous physicians. With the complexity of psychiatric disorders and their mysterious course and etiology, the method of prediction became mostly a trial and error process. However, with the introduction in the early 1950s of increasingly specific medications, such as antipsychotics and antidepressants, interest in more reliable predictive strategies became more pressing. The recognized variability of response to this new class of medications, complicated by the significant heterogeneity of patient samples, puzzled researchers and elevated predictive strategies to high on the list of the research agenda.

By the 1960s, concerns were not just limited to the variability of response to medications, but also included issues related to whether patients would take their medications as prescribed by their doctors. Compliance behaviour and its direct impact on outcomes to treatment became a high priority, based on the clear assumption that the best medications were of no value unless patients would take them. The issue of predicting outcomes and defaulting on taking medications were closely linked. Developing medications that proved to be, at best, partially effective, coupled with defaulting on taking them, initiated for the patient a major clinical crisis related to frequent relapse and the need for hospitalization, creating what became known as the "revolving door phenomenon". Patients who refused or stopped their medications and soon relapsed, requiring hospitalization, were the most expensive component of psychiatric care. In hospitals, as patients became stabilized within a few days, they signed themselves out against medical advice and left the hospital for a short stay in the community, only to relapse again and be re-admitted to hospital. A cycle that can go on for a number of years, leading to a debilitated state of chronicity.

Obviously, having the ability to predict which patients would potentially default on medications would enable clinicians to develop different treatment strategies for those patients. One of the clever strategies that was developed and proven somewhat successful in slowing relapse, was to give medications as an injectable long-acting needle every three to four weeks. But, then some patients would not always consent to such an approach or would simply exercise their right to protest by not showing up for their needle appointments, a complex management challenge. To complicate matters, both a lack of response and a lack of compliance proved to be multifactorial in origin and, as such, both required complex approaches to deal with them.

In 1974, as the challenges escalated, the eminent psychiatrist and psychopharmacologist Professor Leo Hollister published his observations of the state of predictions in psychiatry at that time. His pessimistic conclusion was that chronic disorders would continue to be chronic. Noting that medications were predicted to offer some improvement, based on broad clinical research, he then qualified his response by stating that treatment with medications alone were very unlikely to make someone play the violin if the person had never played before. Truly a guarded assessment of the state of outcomes and their prediction in general.

With such a significant disappointment, not withstanding the ongoing extensive research, another pessimistic report was published in 1978 by two eminent psychiatrists and scientists, Professors Philip May and Solomon Goldberg, who delivered their scientific observation and conclusion of predictions research. Their contribution was in the form of an extensive chapter, included as one of several chapters, in the lengthy 1,731-page book of the seminal and foremost publication regarding the state of psychopharmacology at that time. It was edited by Professors Morris Lipton, Alberto DeMascio and Keith Killam, who delivered the best information of the then current psychopharmacological advances, and also outlined several challenges awaiting resolution. The book Psychopharmacology – A Generation of Progress, as I recall was considered to be the bible for the future of psychopharmacology.

In their extensive and well-balanced review pertaining to the state of prediction in psychiatry, Professors May and Goldberg clearly conclude that the prediction of outcomes using the traditional parameters of demographics, pretreatment status and several other variables, proved of little value in the prediction process. Pondering the reasons for such a negative observation, Professors May and Goldberg questioned whether psychiatric outcomes were inherently unpredictable, or it could possibly be related to the use of inappropriate statistical or design models. In a major shift, the authors suggested a different research path by focusing on events close to the initial course of treatment and, given the early results of the studies by Professors May and Ted Van Putten, applied an early subjective response of neuroleptic induced dysphoria as a reliable predictor of outcome to medication therapy.

As it happened, and to our great surprise, in 1978 we were preparing a brief manuscript about the data from our independent study of early subjective response to antipsychotics and its demonstrated value as a predictor of outcome to medication treatment. Unknown to us, Professor May's group was also researching that area of study. Our investigation was initiated in the mid-1970s, as detailed in my recent 2021 book, by the unexpected suicide of three patients with the diagnosis of schizophrenia. They detested and struggled with taking their medications, claiming that medications had ruined their life. The three patients were young and for a few years prior to their death, they rotated in and out of hospital in what was termed at that time a "revolving door program" at one of the major psychiatric hospitals in Toronto, where I served as the Psychiatrist Director of the program.

An interesting story is worth mentioning, regarding our first manuscript about the phenomenon of subjective tolerability to medications and the noted state of neuroleptic induced dysphoria, as a learning lesson for researchers in the early years of their research career. As it turned out, after we submitted the manuscript to one of the well-known psychiatric journals, it was not long when we received a polite response from the editor informing us the manuscript was declined. The note of decline included comments by the reviewers, who considered the topic of subjective tolerability by patients as a predictor of outcome to medication treatments as no more than "a soft science". Such an early rejection could have scuttled our project, except for our persistence and strong conviction based on the unfortunate and tragic death of the patients in my department, who had bitterly complained about their dislike of medications. Fortunately, the manuscript was picked up by another well-known journal. I was glad, and the moral to this story of prediction is persistence pays off.

Meanwhile, in a later definitive neuroimaging SPECT study we uncovered the neurobiological basis of the phenomenon, as related to the level of the dopamine transmitter in the striatum region of the brain. It also provided new insights, by uncovering why many persons with schizophrenia and on medications take to comorbid abuse of drugs and stimulants in general, such as coffee and smoking. With the discovery of the neurobiological origin of comorbid addiction to be related to the same dopamine region in the brain striatum, we were able to connect the dots and demonstrate the link between neuroleptic-induced dysphoria and comorbid drug addictions, a discovery that aided in improving drug treatments of such patients with significant comorbid drug abuse and employing medications that have low dopamine blocking properties. Using strong dopamine blockers tends to enhance the vulnerability of comorbid drug abuse by further depressing the already low dopamine function in the brain striatum. In the end, subjective tolerability to antipsychotics has been confirmed by other research groups as a predictor of outcomes, as well as a predictor of vulnerability to addictive behaviour in medicated patients with schizophrenia.

Though interest in prediction research became heightened during the 1960s and 1970s, it proved not to be enough to constitute a clear and consistent strategy. The early 1990s was the point in time in which we began to think about holding a working conference, by bringing together a multidisciplinary group of experts in the field to chart the future of prediction research in psychiatry. The idea of the conference, shared by myself and Professor Wolfgang Gaebel, was based not only on concerns about the slow progress of the field, but also to capitalize on the evolving momentum of rising clinical and research interests in the field of prediction psychiatry. The two day conference was convened late in the fall of 1993 in Dusseldorf, Germany, as a central location and in response to Professor Gaebel's kind invitation to host it. The faculty of the two day conference represented the top tier of experts at the time. The agenda allowed for plenty of time for discussion and exchanges between the speakers themselves, and between the speakers and attendees.

The state of prediction at that time was well captured by Professor W. Kopcke from the Institute of Medical Information and Biomathematics in Munster, Germany, in response to a comment and question posed by Professor H-J Moller from Munich, about whether before coming to the question of individual prognosis, must we have a valid and reliable prognosis, with respect to group differentiation? An interesting response from Professor Kopcke was as follows: "If we look outside the window one notices that we are in the autumn season. All of us know that in autumn, leaves fall down from the trees, but we cannot predict for a specific leaf when it will fall down. One can only give the probability, but if such a probability is true for a specific leaf, we do not know if it is also true for other leaves". Indeed, an interesting and challenging response by Professor Kopcke, which was not much different than the statement made long ago by William Shakespeare in Macbeth: "If you can look into the seeds of time, and say which grain will grow and which will not, speak then to me" A clear description of how little psychiatry predictions have changed since Shakespeare's time.

Fortunately, an interesting presentation on the second day of the Dusseldorf conference, given by Professor James Kennedy from the University of Toronto, delivered a note of hope and promise as he reported on his early days in the field of pharmacogenetics.

His intriguing work has served as the foundation of the later major development of pharmacogenomics, benefiting from the extensive information generated by "The Human Genome Project", which will be discussed in the following chapter.

Overall, then, the Dusseldorf meeting proved to be a great success in enhancing the momentum for the renewed interest in prediction research in psychiatry and by forging several collaborations and the pursuit of novel approaches, based on the application of evolving information technology, such as artificial intelligence and big data analytics. As a land mark event, the proceedings of the Dusseldorf conference was published and widely distributed under the title "Prediction of Neuroleptic Treatment Outcome in Schizophrenia – Concept and Methods". The book, edited by myself and Professor Gaebel, was published by Springer-Virlag/Wien in 1994.

b) What is Pharmacogenomics?

Pharmacogenomics is the study of the characteristics of DNA and RNA molecules that impact gene functions that can be influenced by other environmental factors, in contrast to pharmacogenetics, which deals with single genes most often based on the cytochrome P450; the enzyme involved in the breakdown and metabolism of several medications, mostly in the liver. The advent of pharmacogenomics has been based on years of research in the field of genetics and medical technology, culminating in the discovery of the full human genome, as described in an earlier chapter. This major accomplishment has been facilitated by the information provided through the use of modern information technologies, such as AI and big data analytics.

To illustrate the important role of liver enzymes in the metabolism of medications and how much of it reaches the final destination; the brain receptor site, it may prove helpful to schematically follow the course of a swallowed pill in its long transit through the body, a scheme that we published in 1989. After a medication has been swallowed, it finds its way through the gut, where it is broken down into smaller molecules that can be absorbed. For a long time, until recently, the gut was not believed to play a major role beyond the process of breaking down food into smaller molecules and their eventual absorption. Recently, the role of the gut in the metabolism of medications has been receiving more research attention, as a result of the newly and widely recognized role of the gut enzymes in influencing the metabolic process, starting in the gut. The absorbed molecules reach the circulation system and pass through the liver, where the major metabolic process takes place, employing a complex system of enzymes that have different metabolic capabilities, ranging from initiation to induction and acceleration.

Pharmacogenomics is most often based on the cytochrome P450, mostly in the liver, which involves genes coding for the production of cytochrome P450. It is interesting to note that the majority of medications in use in psychiatry are dealt with by no more than seven to ten known types of enzymatic systems, though the P450 system is the most prominent of them. Achieving effective plasma levels, the metabolized products of the medications have to cross the blood/brain barrier to impact on a receptor site within cells that ultimately involve an impact on biological functions, that eventually lead to a behavioural and psychological medications effect. But before its final expression in behaviour, such a response is modulated by the patient's subjective interpretation of the physiological impact. It is certainly a long, complex and well coordinated course through the body, starting from the mouth and gut and ending in the excretion of the metabolic end products, mostly through the kidneys or bowels.

It is also important to note that each stage of this lengthy process can be modified by long-term characteristics of the individual, including genetic factors, and by immediate environmental differences such as diet, prior exposure to the medication, or the effect of other medications. In other words, the response can be modified by the context in which medications are taken, as well as the strength of the therapeutic relationship; an important state that I termed in previous publications as the "extra pharmacological" factor. Such complexity and multiplicity of the different sites where the process can be altered, inevitably could present an element of risk and vulnerability. That is also where the new information technologies can prove helpful, by utilizing information generated by big data analysis.

In recent years, thanks to progress in informatics, major efforts have been directed by the understanding of the various characteristics of the limiting enzymatic system in the liver, particularly in how genetically they are susceptible to variations called "polymorphism". That is where pharmacogenetics and pharmacogenomics can play a major role in screening for such polymorphisms, as an early step in matching medications to the individual genetic characteristics. It all wonderfully and painlessly starts with a simple swab of the mouth, then computers take over until the end results are revealed through complex computations and algorithms. It is truly a major accomplishment that can bring psychiatry much closer to "precision psychiatry" and personalized healthcare, all greatly enabled by the recent advances of informatics such as AI and big data analysis. With such eminent developments that can revolutionize psychiatric treatments, it is appropriate, then, to raise the question that has given the title to this book; Can artificial intelligence and big data analytics save the future of psychiatry?

Imagining Psychiatry in the Era of Artificial Intelligence and Big Data

"Uphill Challenge" 1986
by the author A. G. Awad,
Oil on canvas board 20"x 25"

Imagining the future of psychiatry in the coming years, during a rapidly evolving era of artificial intelligence and big data analytics, is more than simple guessing, since several of its aspects are already present. It means that we have a real and more certain baseline to start from, which makes the predictive and imaginative process of the future much more objective and easier, but only for the short term. Imagining the long-term future in such a quickly evolving field has its limitations and is likely to be no more than guessing or wishful thinking. What tends to complicate matters in the prediction process is the frequent and rapid introduction of more powerful computers that progressively do far more than their previous iteration. Once a powerful generation of computers is introduced, the field is already behind and awaiting the next even more powerful generation of computers. In practice, that means that more accelerated developments both in science and other applications become available. This ultimately raises the uneasy question of whether we are getting closer to an era of the hypothesized supercomputer, with its extra powerful system and whose creators are able to tame and maintain control.

One of the many pressing questions posed immediately is whether such an extraordinary machine can acquire its own mind. Though this question is still in the realm of theory, it is frequently raised in the media and science circles. An example of this concern was posed in a recent special weekend edition of the British Financial Times under the provocative headline: "The Mind: Inside the life of the mind, from Donald Trump's lies, to the science of sleep and AI". This supplement included a number of interesting and challenging contributions about the future, provided by well-known scientists, neuroscientists and futurists. Among them was an interesting contribution by the well-known neurosurgeon, prolific neuroscience writer and humanist Professor Henry Marsh, with the provocative title: "Can We Ever Build a Mind?". It is an ancient quest that has eluded generations of philosophers and scientists, who are still basically debating the question: What is mind?

Though the term "mind" is widely used and frequently talked about, it remains an enigma. Not surprisingly, there exists many definitions for what the mind is. The most simple definition, the one I like most, recognizes the "mind" as an ongoing construction of the brain, the body and the environment (both internal and external) with other related issues, such as consciousness and self-awareness. In other words it is a subjective concept, not a physical entity, uniquely individualistic in nature and closely related to subjective issues such as consciousness and self-awareness. It is the sum total of "me" and "you" as unique individuals, and is rapidly changeable from moment to moment. Since the mind is defined by activities related to the brain, such as thinking, feeling, sensation and perception, it is clear that the brain is the organ of the body in which the mind resides. This is a logical assumption, since such a complex construct as the mind cannot arise or reside in thin air. And so the debate continues, but without a clear resolution in sight.

In Professor Henry Marsh's contribution to the Financial Times supplement, he raises the rhetorical, yet valid question of whether we can construct a mind. His qualified affirmative answer is hedged on the possibility and capability of building supercomputers. Since such a development is anyone's guess, all that is certain is that even if it is possible, it is a very long way away. In other words, such an issue will continue to be one of the known unknowns. Though it may be far away in the future when it happens, it will certainly have a serious and significant impact.

However, with the way science and technology are advancing so rapidly, the future may be not that far away. Just a few days ago, precisely on June 12, 2022, several news media carried a breaking science report, following an interview by the Washington Post with one of Google's engineers named Blake Lemoine, who has been working for several years with Google's program LaMDA-AI (Language Model for Dialogue Applications). Mr. Lemoine claimed that Google's LaMDA chatbot has become sentient, meaning it has developed self-awareness, feelings and self expression. In his published reports, Mr. Lemoine included a sample of his chats. The Washington Post reporter was, herself, able to join the chat. Mr. Lemoine compared his LaMDA chatbot as similar to chatting with a seven to eight year old child, meaning also that the system is not yet fully developed.

In the span of one day, after such interesting and alarming news was released, intense scientific arguments for and against Mr. Lemoine's conclusions erupted and will likely continue on as a heated scientific puzzle. Whether one agrees or disagrees with Mr. Lemoine's conclusions about machines having already developed sentience or not, the reality is that such a state is becoming rapidly closer to being realized. Regardless of the science and its ominous downside, Mr. Lemoine has been suspended by Google, his employer of several years, with the reason being that he broke the company's rule of confidentiality. So much for the germane issue of transparency. Altogether, this rapidly breaking news demonstrates how uncertain and risky long-term predictions can be in a field such as AI, where advances can happen in days rather than years.

As for concerns and lamentations, I will steer away from long-term imaginative predictions of the state of AI and informatics and limit my imaginative predictions to no more than the next ten years, up to the year 2032. By the year 2032, I do believe that AI and big data analytics will have already appropriated a much stronger presence in medical healthcare, but not substantially in the psychiatric field. The development of various medical algorithms will have improved to closely match the designed purpose for which they are intended to be used. New medical computational models, theories and concepts will have been developed and become entrenched in several medical fields, such as medical-imaging, cardiology, ophthalmology, etc. They will also permeate throughout training curricula, in line with the bold recommendations adopted in early 2022 by the Royal College of Physicians and Surgeons of Canada, regarding better integration of AI technology in clinical practice, as detailed in a previous chapter. In psychiatry, as expected, progress will proceed at a slower rate in general and likely will continue that way until new generations of young psychiatrists have been trained and educated according to the recommendations of the Canadian Royal College, when progress will accelerate. With that view, there will be a revival of the rather earlier idea of developing a dedicated college for psychiatry, which continues to be resisted by the power of the current status quo.

On the other hand, the clear endorsement of the RCPSC for the integration of new information technologies, both in medical practice and medical training, seems to add strong support for the serious reformation of the training curricula. Gradual changes in the composition of medical and psychiatric teams have been noted by adding an expert member in medical informatics. Several well-functioning research consortia that include academics and private sector organizations have emerged, with widely noted professional participation that seems to drive research efforts to maximize benefits from various applications of AI technology. The beginning of the creation of a new medical subspecialty in medical informatics is already in place, particularly in such fields as medical imaging, ophthalmology, gastroenterology, cardiology and several others. In psychiatry, the issue of such subspecialization continues to be fraught with debate and challenges related to the need for redefining the role of the psychiatrist, particularly with regard to the role of the general psychiatrist.

Meanwhile, mainstream medical and psychiatric journals have been allocating a more regular publishing space to the field of medical informatics. In psychiatry, the very early identification of potential "markers" has created more pressure to reform the diagnostic classificatory system, shifting away from the traditional symptom-based classification and moving to include other biological and dimensional approaches that cut through several disease entities. One of the major accomplishments and significant changes has been noted in the development of predictive strategies, specifically in the field of pharmacogenomics, which has been rolled out in several countries. This major development is perceived as a landmark step towards the advancement of precise psychiatry and personalized treatment strategies.

Overall, though psychiatry was slow in embracing the new information technology, the clear support and guidance by the RCPSC decision for the integration of informatics in clinical practice, seems to have facilitated the process and it is evolving, being perceived as the champion of such a move. The heated debates and the split in attitudes and opinions among psychiatrists have shrunk, aided by the clear guidance of the RCPSC, in terms of how to manage the transformation process equitably, as well as by the noticeable significant progress in other medical specialties. As a sign of this transformation, several well-known psychotherapy authorities, such as Professor Christopher Fairborn from Oxford University, who recently spoke in Toronto during a conference about the future of psychotherapy, along with several other academics who have endorsed and welcomed the new technology. It is seen as a way to the enhanced future of psychotherapy, through broader dissemination and the ability to develop creative new models for its delivery.

In essence, then, during a ten year period, there has been slow but noticeable progress. The ease of organizing the psychiatric services and having an almost completely digital approach has allowed for the development of creative advancements that allow for the introduction of better access and quality. Psychiatrists have more time to see their patients, a time that has been largely freed from the task of extensive documentation and the demands of the clinical records. More precision in the description of psychiatric symptoms and a trend towards its standardization has been noted. The real potential of identifying biological predictors is adding more optimism and impetus to revise the classificatory system, making it more valid and reliable.

Another important aspect is already within reach; the introduction of information accumulated from widely used wearable devices into the mainstream medical system, a gap that has been lacking for years. By aligning the rapidly proliferating wearable gadgets and incorporating their measuring tools with the healthcare system, it is expected to generate real time information by capturing patients' subjective reports of their symptoms and feelings, which can improve diagnostics and treatments. The enormity of the use of such wearable devices can also contribute to the reliable collection of big data sets, which is one of the key drivers in the psychiatric computational field.

The recently introduced "computational psychiatry", with its emphasis on the rapid and effective translation of neuroscience research into clinical practice, seems to be gaining momentum, reducing the amount of time it takes from research bench to bedside care. It provides a deeper degree of scientific backing for the psychiatrist and psychiatric practice, which has been lacking and eroding the role of psychiatrists for many years. Lastly, and most significantly, the rolling out of the pharmacogenomics program can revolutionize psychiatric treatment and move psychiatry toward a more precise healthcare practice. It is a stimulating development, equivalent to the excitement experienced in the psychiatric community over seventy years ago when Chlorpromazine was introduced in the early 1950s.

On the other hand, definitely we have not yet achieved the kind of future imagined by a number of medical futurists, such as that predicted by Professor Michael Snyder of the Stanford Center for Genomics and Personalized Medicine. In an interview by the New York Times science writer Carl Zimmer in May 2019, Professor Snyder envisioned doctors ordering more than lab tests, checking patients' vital signs and scrutinizing their genome for risk factors. By doing so, doctors of the future can identify diseases and treat them before the early symptoms appear. At the press of a button, the doctor acquires a full history and recent investigations on a monitor. By another press of a button, the doctor can be in contact globally with several other doctors who may have seen similar presentations and discuss how they were dealt with. A utopian vision or a real expectation?

I believe it is for real, and the truth is that several aspects of this futuristic scenario are already here. It may not unfold exactly as envisioned by Professor Snyder, but certainly the essence of it is currently available and has been introduced into practice. The process of attaining such precision technology has been a major scientific feat that has been accomplished through years of creativity, persistence and dedication towards improving our life, and through the hard work of many scientists and the sacrifices they've made. Such major accomplishments also signal the changing times. Discoveries by a single individual or a single group is not possible anymore in our exceedingly complex world. A much more feasible and potentially more successful method is the multidisciplinary, national and international collaborative approach.

The Big Question: Can Artificial Intelligence Deep Machine Learning and Big Data Analytics Save the Future of Psychiatry?

My clear answer in response to the title of this chapter is: Yes...but not alone.

The reason for my qualified response has to do with the need for similar progress to be accomplished in a number of other related fields. Our understanding of the impact of psycho-social and environmental issues on mental health needs to expand, to include such issues as the impact of poverty and economic disparities, stigma and exclusion, the value of connections, relationships and social cognition. Medical philosophy has to be reintroduced and expanded with a greater presence of ethics.

Why would I endorse a positive role for information technology in the future of psychiatry? For several reasons, when approaching the subject through the perspective of my varied experience as a psychiatrist, a clinician, a researcher and a neuroscientist. As a clinician I am particularly aware and burdened by the inadequacy and limitations of psychiatric treatments. Practicing in a fragmented service model that is not strongly backed by hard science is eroding our professional confidence, as well as contributing to the feeling of not being adequately trained or well equipped to deal with future challenges. As a psychiatrist and manager, I have often been disappointed by shortages in psychiatric human resources and the frequent loss of the opportunity to attract the brightest of medical students to choose a career in psychiatry. As a researcher and neuroscientist, the very slow progress in etiological clarifications of major mental disorders is a serious challenge, leaving psychiatrists to provide only partly effective treatments. Diagnostics and classificatory challenges can frequently compromise research efforts. The split of psychiatry from neurology and the inadequacy of training in neurology has left many psychiatrists unable to connect behaviour to brain function. The recent development of behavioural neurology over-shadowing neuropsychiatry widens the gap and wastes expertise and resources, while awaiting an endeavour toward integration.

All in all, I believe the role of the psychiatrist has been eroded by the unmet needs of science and practice. After all, it is a major disappointment that all reforms over the years have not managed to secure a more effective future for psychiatry. I have to admit that I am not an expert in technology, but I certainly understand it and follow it closely. I am particularly interested in new information technology and how it has already provided benefits for other medical specialists. Psychiatry is a discipline of medicine and needs to follow the progressive and bold recommendations of the Royal College of Physicians and Surgeons of Canada, in integrating information technology and digital approaches with clinical practice.

The near completion and imminent rolling out of pharmacogenomic approaches in psychiatry is a major step forward. The advanced technology that allowed for its extensive proliferation are smart phones, along with the many wearable gadgets and devices that have opened the door to integration into medical practice. This development can improve our ability to obtain live minute-to-minute information from patients, which will certainly improve outcomes and contribute to the collection of information for big data analytics and the search for reliable biomarkers. At present, as in previous times, there are no fail-proof guarantees for the success of a new approach, but what we already know is encouraging and inviting to try a path that has never been followed before. I am enthusiastic and feel more confident about the future, based not only on how much the new information technology has offered medicine, but also by the extensive benefits we accrue from it in our daily lives, from cell phones to paying e-bills, etc. For sure, there is no future without an inherent risk to be recognized and included in the risk benefit assessment of major future plans.

PART B

Other Challenges and Controversies – Phenomenological and Nosological Challenges

Part B1: Neuropsychiatry, Behavioural Neurology and the Inevitable Meeting of Minds

The recent development of "behavioural neurology" as a sub-specialty of neurology has taken several psychiatrists by surprise and concern, lamenting the appropriation by neurology of several core principles of our neuropsychiatry. On the other hand, this recent development succeeded in opening the often raised, but not seriously pursued question of what separates neurology and psychiatry. Interestingly enough, both disciplines inhabit one organ: the brain. The dualism of mind and body that has separated the two fields over the last century has left neurology to deal with issues related to the integrity of the nervous system, while psychiatry was assigned to deal with issues related to the mind. From time to time, as happened recently, such issues come to a sharp focus regarding whether this separation serves the interests of patients on both sides of the divide. As has happened many times over the last few decades, the debate ended without a serious resolution and both fields continued their independent, but ambiguous situation, confirming their already widely split state. In any case, and regardless of which side one represents, both sides of the debate concluded that close collaboration and convergence to be the most desirable approach to serve our clinical and academic agendas.

That was the case up until the recent development of the one-sided decision to create behavioural neurology as a rather new sub-specialty of neurology. Something there seemed to touch the sensibility of such a split at a time when the evolving neuroscience field, shared by both fields, had been noted to make significant strides, aided by the major advances in the fields of neuroimaging and molecular biology. We are now at an unprecedented time, having the tools that allow us a window on the inner functioning of the brain. At the same time, clinical observation seems to impose its reality, the noted frequency of behavioural consequences of brain neural disorders that require more understanding and more skills to deal with them.

Meantime, psychiatry is maturing and getting over the period of the psychoanalytic dogma, returning back slowly to the mainstream fold of experimental medicine. The extensive historic genetic and family studies of the early 1960s, clearly confirmed the biological origins of major psychiatric disorders as impacted upon by a host of environmental and psychosocial issues. The introduction of the first specific antipsychotic medication Chlorpromazine in the early 1950s, and the subsequent development of other psychoactive medications, though far from perfect have merged to consolidate a biological reality in the context of the bio-psychosocial strategy. With all the modern advances, why is it that the relationship between neurology and psychiatry has been less than amicable for almost a century and at times contentious and antagonistic, and quite often failed due to misunderstandings and historic biases.

For me personally, I recognized for the first time the unfriendly state and ambiguous relationship of psychiatry and neurology in the 1960s when I was in Rome, Italy, completing my year of post-doctoral fellowship at the Institute of Health Research. At that time, both Rome, Paris and almost all of Europe were besieged by radical and violent demonstrations that threatened the status quo. In Rome, the state of anarchy lead to major violence and the assassination of Aldo Moro, the Prime Minister of Italy. Among the demands of the demonstrators was the push for closure of all psychiatric hospitals and shutting down psychiatry as a medical system. In Paris, the demonstrators occupied the Sorbonne University, including the office of the influential Chairman of the Department of Neuropsychiatry, Professor Jean Delay, who carried the title of Professor of Neurology and Psychiatry. The violent demonstrators and the occupants of Professor Jean Delay's office were adamant anti-psychiatry zealots. To make a long story short, under tremendous pressure Professor Delay had to abandon the dual title of Professor of Neurology and Psychiatry, ushering in the split of both medical disciplines. For those interested, the details of this violent story is well documented in a very interesting book by Professor Driss Moussaoui titled "A Biography of Jean Delay", published in 2002.

Such a brutal story was in reality the first knowledge I had of the politics of the relationship between psychiatry and neurology. At the same time, a similar relationship was developing miles away in the United States. In 1969, I made my way to Canada and eventually joined psychiatry, but a few years prior to that, in 1965, the US Residency Review Committee of Psychiatry and Neurology (RCC) decided to delete psychiatric training as a mandatory experience for neurologists. That was the beginning of the unravelling of the mutual training relationship between psychiatry and neurology. Though such a major decision was not the result of violent acts, as in Paris, nevertheless it was the climax of a misunderstood and highly acrimonious relationship between both disciplines, that further confounded the already existing split. As I recall, at the time I started my psychiatry practice in the early 1970s, the relationship between psychiatry and neurology can best be described as both disciplines being keen on their independence and each going their own way. Neither meddled in the other's affairs, leading to an unsatisfactory state that undermined clinical practice and impeded academic collaboration.

To navigate my way in understanding the origins of the less than friendly relationship between psychiatry and neurology, I consulted voluminous amounts of literature that clearly outlined the shades of grey in such a broad divide. Focusing on recent reviews, three major contributions proved of great help in not only documenting the history, but also clearly identifying possible pathways in dealing with the unacceptable divide. Chronologically, the first contribution was by three professors from Harvard Medical School in Boston: Professors Bruce Price, Raymond Adams and Joseph Coyle, published in the year 2000 in the journal "Neurology", which is the publication of the American Academy of Neurology. The excellent review had the appropriate title "Neurology and psychiatry – closing the great divide", written by the three authors who were each engaged in both neurology and psychiatry. The brief historical review detailed how psychiatry and neurology began together and was accepted by most of the senior academics in the nineteenth century and beyond, and carried the dual title of Professor of Psychiatry and Neurology, exemplified by the contributions of such academics as Pick, Korsakoff, Alzheimer and many others. By the early twentieth century, several neurologic syndromes had been clinically defined and their neuropathology was clearly identified. Psychiatry, on the other hand, pursued disorders of mind for which there was no demonstrable pathology, being described as idiopathic or functional disorders. Hence the split into "organic versus functional" gained ground in making the gap between psychiatry and neurology much wider.

It is interesting that in a much earlier reference, it was claimed that neurology did not arise from psychiatry, but instead from internal medicine. The fact is, the medical staff of the ancient mental asylums, at least in Britain, were provided with physicians who were interested in anatomic- and neuropathology. Documented in the late eighteenth century, during a conflict between the superintendent and a group of physicians providing care at one of the major mental asylums, the superintendent accused them of only being interested in pursuing their anatomical and psychopathological interests instead of providing care for their patients. In the end, the physicians resigned and became the early founders of a physician group that eventually became the British Association of Neurology.

As neurology moved forward, psychiatry slowly moved away and adopted the emerging Freudian psychoanalysis, particularly in the US. This new doctrinaire approach in psychiatry managed to move psychiatry away from its roots in biology and experimental medicine, however, a small group of psychiatrists persisted in their belief that psychiatric disorders were brain disorders. Eventually, by the end of the Second World War, with biological and pharmacological advances of the time the psychoanalytic dogma started to wane, but the ambivalent relationship between neurology and psychiatry continued. An interesting statement by Dr. Francis Braceland, who was the president of the American Board of Psychiatry and Neurology in the early 1960s, while reflecting on how much animosity had coloured the relationship between neurology and psychiatry, he said, "to get neurologists and psychiatrists of that period to sit down together without police present was in itself an accomplishment". During that time several old historical biases confounded the mutual relationship. Psychiatrists acknowledged that neurologists knew about the brain, but not about the mind, while neurologists believed that psychiatrists knew about the mind, but not about the brain.

Fortunately, such a mutual distrust has been giving way to their complementary roles in recent decades, aided by the evolving new medical technologies and the rapid advances in neuroscience. The pathway that the three Harward authors recommended for change was through a major revision of the training curricula on both sides. It is interesting that in their concluding remarks, Professor Price and his colleagues quote the words of Professor Freud in 1920, about his abandonment of trying to develop an anatomic physiological model for the mind until a time came when scientific methods would be sufficiently developed to allow for the construction of such a model.

He added that the "deficiencies in our description (his psychoanalytic concepts) would probably vanish if we were already in a position to replace the psychological terms with the physiological or chemical ones". I agree with the sentiment of the three eminent authors, that we are slowly approaching such a state. And that is one of the reasons I believe that the dichotomy of mind and body will likely begin to fade.

One of the other two major reviews that I greatly benefited from during the writing of this chapter was by Professor Joseph Martin, the past dean of Harvard's Medical School in 2002, with the title "The integration of neurology, psychiatry, and neuroscience in the 21st century". As a neurologist, Professor Martin's recommendations for integration have been and continue to be relevant to our times. His paper adds a significant voice to the need for redesigning the education of future psychiatrists and neurologists. The third review was by Professor Michael Fitzgerald from Cambridge University, recently published in 2018, with the provocative title "Do psychiatry and neurology need a close partnership or a merger?". Reflecting on such a serious and important question posed by Professor Fitzgerald, my response is to ask another important question; are we ready for a full blown merger at the present time? My answer is certainly a clear "no".

As I mentioned earlier, any kind of merger, even those mergers that include obvious benefits or are unavoidable by necessity, usually encompass a high degree of risk and feelings of loss. The loss of identity and the ways of practice that we are accustomed to is inevitable. It also involves a change of professional relationships. The reality is that in any successful merger, the eventual sum has to be bigger than the individual components entered in the merger. In general, mergers at best are a highly emotional process that is based on history and the type of work that generally defines us. For a successful merger, one has to enter into a challenging process from a clear point of strength. One of the major strengths in psychiatry is its adoption of the biopsychosocial model, which moved psychiatry not only closer to science and the humanities, but also defined the pathway for the future. Yet, in spite of the recognized influence and importance of the biopsychosocial model, it is still not yet fully entrenched nor fully practiced. In reality, in spite of its attractiveness it is still a work in progress, attempting to fill the void left by the unravelling of several decades of psychoanalytic dogma. In neurology, work with the biopsychosocial model has barely started, as neurologists have continued to struggle with finding a place to begin.

For these reasons, I do not think we should engage in a rather risky project we are not yet ready for nor clear about its potential benefits. I am more comfortable proposing another approach that involves a limited targeted merger. Looking into the issues that bind us, rather than divide us, the recent development by neurology of the discipline of behavioural neurology might provide the opportunity for a meeting of the minds, leading to the development of a combined third discipline side-by-side with neurology and psychiatry: the discipline of "clinical neuroscience". There would be fewer challenges there, since neuropsychiatrists and behavioural neurologists speak the same language, use the same narratives and concepts, and they both use the same tools. It is clear that such a process cannot be accomplished without major reforms and a reshaping of the training curricula; the core training for both psychiatrists and neurologists should include rotations in the newly developed "clinical neuroscience". It is worth noting that over the past two years, an admirable effort was made by a few leaders of both psychiatry and neurology in developing a global curriculum that encompasses principles from behavioural neurology and neuropsychiatry, which is a good starting point.

In the end, creation of the new discipline "clinical neuroscience" as the route of a targeted merger, would be a practicable and viable path for its achievement. It certainly will not succeed as a major project unless a number of influential and progressive champions guide and support the process, and shepherd it to its ultimate objective. Just a hope towards a better future for both psychiatry and neurology and, more importantly, for our patients on both sides of the divide.

The Subjective/Objective Dichotomy – Relevance to Nosology, Research and Clinical Practice

In the history of modern psychiatry, the 1960s stands out as one of the major progressive and optimistic periods, following the successful introduction of the first specific antipsychotic medication Chlorpromazine in the early 1950s. Though it was not long before it was recognized that Chlorpromazine and similar medications proved to be imperfect, this new antipsychotic discovery managed to usher in a significant era of modern psychiatry, allowing for broad and important developments in both clinical psychiatric practice and research efforts that strengthened the early roots of neurobiology in psychiatric practice. As part of this enlightened period, significant efforts were made to standardize observations and diagnoses, by developing new rating scales and revising the classificatory system of diagnoses. The objective was to improve psychiatric practice and psychiatric research methodologies, in support of the rapidly evolving psychobiological research strategies that could provide the potential for psychiatry to become a stronger scientific medical discipline.

Attempts to objectify observations were commendable and very desirable, but these accomplishments were attained at a high price: a noticeable decline of interest in the patients' subjective world. What our patients told us about their inner feelings and their experiences with illness and their treatment, though acknowledged by their attending psychiatrist, was usually ignored or assigned a secondary order, in the context of other issues that were deemed to be more objective and high in the value of establishing a diagnosis or revising treatments. The patients' subjective complaints of how they feel on medications were received by physicians with some doubts and suspicions and considered to be part of their illness state. The irony of such paradox has been that clinicians were ready to accept patients' reports as the basis for diagnosis, but at the same time clinicians were suspicious and reluctant regarding the reliability of the same patients' reports of how they feel subjectively about medications or their illness experience. A truly worrisome situation.

As I documented and detailed in my 2021 book, "The Search for a New Psychiatry", we tragically lost three young patients with schizophrenia to suicide, as a result of not paying adequate attention to their bitter subjective complaints of how they hated to take medications, and we lacked a better alternative. The most telling of such a tragic story, and also the scientific attitude at that time, was the reflection of a brief clinical report we submitted to one of the major psychiatric journals. In no time, we received a decline notice that included some of the reviewer's comments, as well as the view that researching subjective states in psychiatry was a sort of "soft science". It took a high level of persistence and deep conviction to ignore the reviewer's negative comments and continue our research project, providing proof of the concept and finally shepherding it to its conclusion: the neurobiological clarification of why some patients disliked their psychiatric medication and hated taking it, with subsequent frequent relapses and costly re-hospitalizations.

In the end, thanks to technological advances in neuroimaging, we were able to finally demonstrate that such serious dysphoric responses to antipsychotics were related to the level of dopamine functioning in the striatal region of the brain. Firstly, these patients had low dopamine levels in their striatum, that was further lowered by giving them medications that decreased their striatal dopamine functioning. In addition, such low dopamine levels in the striatum managed to clarify the well-known observation of why many patients on medications such as the Chlorpromazine type, tended to have a significant vulnerability in developing comorbid drug abuse problems. Now we clearly understand how and why some patients feel worse on certain strong dopamine-blocking medications. As we documented, the nature of their unpleasant feelings was related to dysphoric responses to the medication, which was not just effective in altering mood, but also included serious motor and cognitive components that made their response much more intolerable and confusing. The moral of this tragic account is that by ignoring patients' subjective complaints, we would not have been able to improve their treatment that lead to better outcomes.

I do believe that the decline in interest in exploring the subjective world of our patients is a serious and worrisome omission, drawing significant critical comments by several academics. One of the passionate critics of this a decline was Professor Herman Van Praag, who lamented this undesirable situation and passionately expressed his important message in a 1992 contribution in the British Journal of Psychiatry, under the title, "Reconquest of the Subjective: Against the Waning of Psychiatric Diagnosing". A few years earlier, the distinguished psychiatrist and humanist Professor John Strauss from Yale University, warned the field of psychiatry that by ignoring the subjective experience of our patients, descriptive psychiatry could be seriously limited, along with our ability to understand and optimally manage our patients. One of his major and interesting contributions had to do with how one can fully understand or feel what it is like to be in the mind of another person. One of the interesting anecdotes of how Professor Strauss felt about this question was his response, to take up acting, though he never had the training for it. It was his way of getting close to understanding how it feels to be in the mind of someone else. I certainly owe him a good deal of appreciation in guiding me in the early years, at a time when I was struggling to prove the importance of paying attention to the subjective world of our patients and how to dispel the erroneous notion of it being "soft science".

I do believe the current state of knowledge in psychiatry is lacking clear and reliable etiological diagnostic markers. And in such situation, we are not entitled to ignore or reject our patients' subjective experiences. In reality, I do believe that measuring symptoms using a scale may qualify as a good standardization, but it's not necessarily being more objective. The clinical reality is that we have to rely diagnostically on what patients tell us. In the majority of psychiatric disorders, as much as we standardize and try to objectify, we still have to rely on information patients give us, which has to be funnelled through the interviewer's subjective interpretation of the scaled observations. By incorrectly labelling these phenomena as "objective" by the interviewer, subjective bias cannot completely be eliminated, nor is it correct to assume that such a process is free from a theoretical or preconceived bias.

In practice, then, the distinction of information into subjective or objective at the current state of knowledge, is mostly theoretical and practically non-existent. Ignoring the subjective is to ignore the whole truth and impose premature closure of any further meaningful exploration, and it also undermines the interest of developing appropriate methodologies to integrate both domains into a meaningful typology. With the current rapid evolution of informatics, such as the use of AI, deep learning and big data analytics, these powerful technologies could provide us with the tools for its successful incorporation. One recent example of patients' subjective response to a new medication, in the context of a formal clinical multi-site trial, showed that using a subjective response such as satisfaction, proved to be the earliest change we were able to pick clinically before any symptomatic changes.

Fundamentally, I believe listening seriously to our patients and taking their views, feelings and concerns seriously, can provide the cornerstone for any meaningful and successful patient-centred care. Such an approach enhances the empowerment of our patients to share in the process of their own recovery, and prevents the care process from becoming dehumanized.

Lunacy and the Moon - Reflections on the Interactions of the Brain and the Environment

If one asks any nurse who has served consistently in the emergency department of any large city hospital, one would get a consistent confirmation of the long held belief that moon activity and its phases can influence not only emotional and psychiatric states, but also impact physical health. During the phase of the full moon the emergency room tends to be in chaos, not just by the number of patients presenting there, but also by the complexity and severity of such presentations that often require hospital admissions. Indeed, a few cursory surveys generally support this notion. On the other hand, most of the scientists, whether astronomers or chronobiologists, seem to doubt any lunar impact. Yet, the notion has persisted for ages since its ancient description by philosophers, beginning in the first century AD, by Aristotle and followed by similar observations by the Roman philosopher Pliny.

One of the earliest theories about the connection of the moon with altered and deranged behaviour was put forward by Pliny, who suggested that the full moon caused an increase in dew to form, which added more moisture to the brain and likely led to madness. Hence, the term "lunatic", which is of Latin origin referring to the moon, was a designation assigned to the widely developed ancient mental asylums. Though never really understood or proven, it is interesting that the idea of increasing moisture in the brain and using the analogy of moon-related tides has resurfaced in recent decades, among a long list of possible hypotheses. In spite of the continued popular and scientific research interests, not a single study yet has been replicated conclusively. Obviously, one has to accept that the absence of evidence does not equal no evidence. In other words, it is possible that with the rapid advances in bio-medical technologies, we may yet be able to better understand such curious observations.

Similar to the well established push and pull of tides related to the phases of the moon, in humans the brain functions in rhythmic patterns, such as the sleep/wake cycles for example, which have directed focus on the role that light plays. One long held hypothesis speculates that full moonlight could disrupt the sleep/wake cycle and have a significant impact on mood and behaviour. Indeed, in recent decades we have been able to appreciate the therapeutic impact of light in clinical situations, such as seasonal mood disorders. Not going into psychopathological states, a simple observation of the impact of light is how the effect of a bright, sunny day can cheer the mood of a normal population during their daily living activities.

One of the interesting observations that I also experienced during an academic visit in the 1990s, with Professor Anne Wirz-Justice in her chronobiology research laboratory, at the Basel Psychiatric Institute in Switzerland. At lunchtime, she and I joined all of her department staff, and congregated outside on the beautiful green grounds of the institute. I was told it was an obligatory routine for everyone to leave their offices and enjoy the weather outside at noon, when the light cycle was at its maximum midday peak. Afterwards, when I spoke with the staff, everyone reported feeling much better and having more vigour to sustain them in their labs through the lengthy afternoon.

Returning back to the affects of the moon, a recent study suggested that sleep varies across different moon phases. Like other similar studies in a highly controlled sleep lab environment, this study was never replicated. One of the critical concerns about many failed studies of this nature has been the lack of a systematic approach to record the sleep patterns of the same individuals over time and over the various phases of the moon. A more recent study that took this criticism seriously in the study design, was reported by Professor Tom Wehr of the Institute of Mental Health, Bethesda, Maryland. Professor Wehr's study included seventeen patients with rapid cycling bipolar disorder and had shown a clear regularity of their episodes. Patients were meticulously followed for years and the data clearly demonstrated precisely when the episodes occurred. One of the interesting results of Wehr's study was the observation that the patients' cycles during a two week period were roughly synchronized with the cycle of the moon-related tides.

Though the study offered no explanation for the synchronized activity, it focused attention on it being related to the electromagnetic forces inherent in the moon-tide gravitational phenomenon. This magnetic theory seems to have its supporters, based on extensive research on fruit flies that have a protein called cryptochrome that appears to function as a magnetic sensor. Cryptochrome is an important component of the molecular clocks that drive the 24-hour circadian rhythms in all cells, including those of the brain. It is a big jump from a fruit fly to the complex human brain, but suffice to say that at the present time the proposed moon's influence on behaviour continues to be unconfirmed and not clearly understood. It is an interesting theory and will continue to be a challenge for future investigation, as it is relevant to the cyclicity in brain functioning, several psychiatric disorders, understanding the impact of shift work and the disruption of normal cycles.

In the end, I have to say that my purpose in bringing forward such an interesting account is not just related to the impact of moon activity on human behaviour, but in reality my purpose is to put particular focus on the issue of environmental impact, in its broadest sense, and its interaction with the brain. I don't mean just climate or planetary influences, but the broad spectrum of daily activities that we are all exposed to, from social connections and interactions, to both rewarding and distressing events. In essence, all issues related to the human condition and how we live and respond to them. How the brain identifies these challenges and prepares to deal with them is in reality a serious challenge awaiting further understanding. It is a challenge for both health and disease, as well as a reminder that the brain itself is not the sole master of the universe, so to speak, but is significantly influenced by a wide variety of environmental states. It is possible that the ancient evolutionary jump from nomadic life and living basically outside in the open, to a type of settled life may have equipped our brains with tools that help in recognizing various environmental challenges and mastering how advantageously the brain responds to them. Meanwhile, until we have a better understanding of these important cyclic events, one is left to enjoy the fascinating influences of the moon in romantic fiction in novels and films, including my favourite movie: Moonstruck.

"Woke Psychiatry"! What is it?

I have to admit from the outset that the term "woke" was not familiar to me, until I heard it repeatedly mentioned on the US media covering the November 2020 US elections. Before that time, I simply recognized it as something to do with the word "wake" and its past tense "woke". The concept of "waking" and "awakening", on the other hand, were part of a familiar psychiatric concept meaning to "return to oneself". The term "awakening" has been used to describe an improved state, following the use of new antipsychotic medications in a class frequently referred to as "second generation antipsychotics". These are compared to the effect and impact of the old generation antipsychotics, such as the original antipsychotic Chlorpromazine, and the many similar ones that followed and produced a state of daze and drowsiness often described by patients as making them feel like a "zombie". The new generation medications were marketed as better and would awaken patients from their zombie state. Though the new medications have proven to be a bit better in reducing certain side effects, unfortunately their state of "awakening" have been compromised by other serious side-effects that continue to be troublesome. Obviously, by the 2020 US elections, the use of the terms "woke", "wake" and "awake" in the political arena had nothing in common with what was meant in psychiatric jargon.

By the year 2021, the term "woke" not only dominated the social and political electronic media, but also managed to infiltrate the medical profession and, even more so, psychiatric discourse. In May 2021, I came across a commentary contributed by a senior psychiatrist in a well-known national conservative newspaper, "The Globe and Mail", under the title "Woke Psychiatrists Have Lost Sight of the Biological Causes of Mental Illness". As expected, this provocative article was followed by a barrage of commentary, both critical and supportive. The heated argument quickly unfolded into a tense political debate about civil rights and the politics of discrimination, which are topics that are not new to psychiatry. However, reflecting on the undertone and reading between the lines, I felt strongly that both sides were missing the central issue. At that point, I asked myself if psychiatry needed to be dragged once more into a rather divisive fight and become a distraction, similar to the anti-psychiatry period of the 1960s. I strongly feel that the challenges for psychiatry at present are not about the social or biological origins of psychiatry. That battle was waged decades ago, and to a large extent reached a reasonable and realistic balance within the clear context of the biopsychosocial model, and has been mostly settled and accepted.

I do believe that the terms "woke" and "wokeness" are, in general, contributing to unnecessary conflicts, which to a large extent is well meaning, but broadly misinterpreted. "Woke" is a very nuanced term that has become charged and weaponized, presenting itself as a new ideology. The term "woke" is African-American vernacular English that has many evolving meanings, ranging from "good" to being almost "racist". The meaning depends on its context, who is saying it and to whom it is said. Not surprisingly, then, the concept of "woke" and "wokeness" has acquired several definitions.

According to the Oxford English Dictionary definition, being "woke" is being alert to injustice in society, especially regarding racism. Wikipedia has a more or less similar meaning, but as an adjective the term "woke" means being alert to racial prejudices and discrimination, originating in the African-American community. On the other hand, others consider wokeness an offensive ideology, with a negative association to those who promote political ideas involving race and identity. This negative interpretation considers being "woke" equivalent to being on the radical left, with all of its conflicting definitions and meanings.

I find that the comments regarding wokeness by the well-known writer and humanist David Brooks, in a 2012 edition of The New York Times, captures its very nature, "Wokeness encompasses the need to search for more knowledge, understanding and the truth in order to challenge injustice". In essence, according to David Brooks' view, wokeness has to be about more than just saying the right words in the right context, which is the definition in the Marian-Webster Dictionary. It lists the term "woke" as the third most used word among the top ten words of the year 2021, as revealed by their annual survey.

According to these definitions, woke is being aware of and actively attentive to important facts and issues, especially with regard to racial and social justice. Emphasizing the activism component seems to have attracted several critical comments by academic professors of psychology. Notable among them is Professor Rupert W. Nacoste, of North Carolina State University, who posted a critique in 2019 in Psychology Today titled "To Be or Not To Be Woke", which I appreciated and highly recommend as a thoughtful and insightful contribution. His astute observation, "...people are quick to show how 'woke' they are by attacking someone else". For me, it is similar to a reminder of what the ancient philosopher Nietzche had warned about centuries ago, "Beware that, when fighting monsters, you yourself do not become a monster...". This old and clear pronouncement still holds true to the present time. I do believe that movements and ideologies, for whatever cause, are susceptible to becoming the thing they despise and criticize.

Which brings me back to the newspaper contribution by my senior colleague. Though I do believe he was likely well-meaning and simply worried and fearful of the return of the 1960s era of anti-psychiatry and labelling mental illness a myth, by now it is clear that mental disorders are real brain disorders and, like all brain functions, are subject to environmental laws and influences, including significant contributions from psycho-social determinants. Fortunately, at its core, psychiatry embodies empathy, compassion and sensitivity, as well as respect for the needs of others, which is above and beyond what "wokeness" is or confers, in the best sense of the term.

The Ignored and Uncommon Psychiatric Disorders and The "Herd" Pattern of Psychiatric Research Interests

The majority of classificatory diagnostic systems, including the DSM, contain a number of rare psychiatric diagnostic states, such as Cotard and Capgras syndromes, and a few others that are mostly culture-bound states. Several other psychiatric conditions, though not included in the list of rare psychiatric conditions, are relatively uncommon, such as catatonia, which was first described in 1874 by the German neuropsychiatrist Karl Ludwig Kahlbaum. At that time, Professor Kahlbaum was the director of the old psychiatric hospital in Gorlitz, Germany. Based on his interest in psychotic disorders, he recorded his extensive observations of cyclic states that had both significant motor and mood components. Kahlbaum collected a broad cluster of such states that presented with a wide range of behaviour, from motor excitement to total immobility, with various shades and grades in between. He called these clusters "catatonia". His detailed description of catatonic symptoms proved to be influential, to the point that it impressed the German psychiatrist Professor Emil Kraepelin, who included such states of catatonia in his concept of dementia praecox. The rationale at that time was that most states of catatonia ended in dementia and death. Since his conclusion, for the next seventy to eighty years the concept of catatonia was completely buried in schizophrenia, meaning it received little research attention on its own.

The recent modern revival of the concept of catatonia owes its beginnings to the modern introduction of better definitions and the development of better measurement tools, such as the widely used Bush-Francis Catatonia Rating Scale, as well as the observed similarity of the state of catatonia to mood disorders. The better characterization of the concept of catatonia led to the inclusion of a number of pathognomonic symptoms, such as immobility, passivity, mutism, negative posturing, cataplexy, waxy flexibility, withdrawal and refusal to eat or drink. The observation that catatonic states can accompany other physical, neurological and metabolic disorders raised considerable doubt about whether catatonia in reality was unique to schizophrenia. One of the major critics for assigning catatonia to schizophrenia has been the American neurologist and psychiatrist Professor Max Fink. In his acerbic 2010 publication in the well known journal "Schizophrenia Bulletin", he firmly emphasized that "catatonia is not schizophrenia". Fink declared that the connection was Kraepelin's error, and he pushed his view of the need for the recognition of catatonia as an independent syndrome, a point of view with which several clinicians and scientists agree.

Although catatonia as a clinical state may have received a good deal of clinical attention, due to its peculiarity and the difficulties encountered in its management, much less is known about its pathophysiology. It is interesting how the few pathophysiological concepts that evolved were perceived more by association, rather than by being parts of an integrated conceptual model. That catatonic states include a motor component, inevitably has led to a hypothesized role for dopamine in the striatum and basal ganglia of the brain. Similarly the observations that benzodiazepines can prove helpful in ameliorating symptoms, posed a possible role for the neurotransmitter GABA. Recent neuroimaging studies suggested a role for a mesolimbic, mesostriatal dopaminergic imbalance. Other studies pointed to a possible role for the frontal lobe of the brain, as in the case of epilepsy accompanied with catatonia. Altogether, then, there is not yet a clear pathophysiological understanding of this rather broad heterogeneous state, and that is where the concept at present is slowly lingering, awaiting the revival of more research interests.

Periodic Catatonia

An uncommon sub-type of catatonia is the state of periodic catatonia, which initially held clinical and research significance, but then similarly faded away to a point that at present many young psychiatrists have never seen a case or been taught any information about it. By definition, periodic catatonia is a puzzling and intriguing syndrome that involves cyclic catatonic states, mostly of the akinetic type, that regularly recurs with completely symptom-free periods in between.

One of the most curious presentations I have attended to, occurring in the early 1980s, was that of Mr. CA, a gentleman in his mid-sixties who was well known to the medical psychiatry program that I managed at a large University of Toronto-affiliated general hospital. As in previous admissions, and almost at the same time of year, Mr. CA was brought to hospital by his family one day in early autumn. He was completely immobile, totally mute and was refusing to eat or take medications. In hospital he would lie passively in bed, completely mute, but seemingly fully conscious. Mr. CA would not respond to any questions or requests, neither by words nor gestures. Yet, he never resisted a physical examination or having his blood pressure checked. Feeding him or giving him medications often proved to be a major challenge for nurses.

On one occasion, after a lot of effort made to feed Mr. CA, the nurse in charge asked me to visit him, as the staff believed that, in spite of his mutism, he seemed to be more comfortable in my presence. As I intervened, he did finally take some food. Interestingly, after his recovery that usually took about three months, I asked him if he remembered the incident. He did clearly recall the incident, explaining humorously that I was the oldest person on the clinical team, of which most of its members were young and included student nurses, psychiatric medical residents and other relatively young staff. He added, "You were the closest in age to me", despite at least a fifteen year difference in our ages.

Even though Mr. CA never displayed aggressive behaviour, in his utter silence and absence of any communication, some of the young nursing staff tended to become easily frustrated with him. One time, a young nurse expressed her unpleasant frustrations while attending to him and, to the surprise of the nurse and many members of the clinical team, after Mr. CA's recovery, he recalled her unpleasant comments, which clearly proved how aware he was of the environment around him. Similar observations have been reported in a few published anecdotal case reports.

In spite of his management difficulties, Mr. CA attained the status of being a "celebrity patient", following an incident of a fire alarm bell continuously ringing on his hospital floor and the public announcement of a fire. As the nurses and other staff rushed to evacuate patients according to the fire alarm response plans, one of the patients that was the first to jump from their bed was Mr. CA, curiously. As the fire was contained and the patients returned to their rooms, Mr. CA lapsed once more into his catatonic state of immobility and mutism. Indeed, it was a curious and puzzling incident that left the psychiatric medical residents wondering whether they were dealing with a condition of malingering, which was not the case. Mr. CA had been seen and fully examined by a number of psychiatric and neurology experts, including EEG recordings and autonomic investigations. Up until the present day, these incidents of his unexpected behaviour are still vivid in my mind and lack any reasonable explanation.

There exists a few anecdotal reports about similar observations, but, unfortunately, there have been no systematic studies of such phenomena, nor for the concept of catatonia in general. For some reason, probably as a result of the uncommon nature of these presentations, research interest in such important neuroscience challenges has been lost. The last serious research effort to understand these peculiar psychiatric states and offer better treatments for periodic catatonia was in the 1960s, conducted by Professor Rolv Gjessing, a well known neuropsychiatrist in Denmark. Professor Gjessing believed that cyclic nitrogen imbalance and thyroid imbalance were major factors behind the development of periodic catatonia. For at least a couple of decades thyroid treatment was tried, but with mixed results. Indeed, Mr. CA was a patient who we tried thyroid treatment on, but with no significant benefit.

Since the extensive studies of Professor Gjessing, there have not been any serious specific research programs for the study of such an uncommon and important neuroscience puzzle. The opportunity to clarify aspects of basic brain functioning or, more precisely, dysfunctional and relatively uncommon presentations gets lost, and the lack of teaching about potentially significant aspects of brain functioning produces psychiatric trainees who are not aware or have any knowledge of such important neuroscience and psychiatric states. Although these unusual states are relatively rare or uncommon, ignoring them might miss the opportunity of keeping them on the research agenda and the important information that would contribute to a more comprehensive knowledge of brain dysfunction.

The En Masse Shifts in Psychiatric Research Patterns

Abrupt shifts in psychiatric research interests have been regularly noted in recent decades. An obvious example has been the focused intense research of what is known as the group of negative symptoms of schizophrenia for at least two or three decades, to the exclusion of other important challenges. Possibly due to frustration and the absence of any significant positive data, as well as dwindling funding, research focus abruptly shifted and moved en mass to cognitive deficits in schizophrenia, where we are approaching yet another new and imminent exit. Another major shift is understandable, considering the impact of limited funding on the face of insubstantial research findings that haven't added much to our current knowledge. Yet, such a quick desertion creates discontinuity and the potential loss of future opportunities that could provide more gains through persistence, or at least to not completely shut the door on important research challenges.

It is a complex and seriously problematic research question, that compels us to review our research plans and policies. I can imagine the frustration of a research project that is going nowhere and the pressure to join what I call the "herd" pattern of moving quickly to another vogue research subject that is consistent with the "taste of the day". Is it possible and more useful to entrust a few experts and well-equipped research centres to be funded for a long enough time to deal with specific research challenges, and not have it tied to the frequent rush to produce publishable papers? Maybe we should go back and revisit some of the important issues that have already been deserted, due to a lack of success at that time, and give them a fresh opportunity using different new technologies and new conceptual thinking. What I really want to say in this chapter is that we clearly need another serious look at research policies, strategies, priorities and their organization, which is sadly a repeat of what many have already said before.

Part B2: Clinical Challenges

Notes on Creativity, Emotions and Psychiatric Disorders

Last year, in my 2021 book that ushered in the theme: The Search for a New Psychiatry, I briefly touched on the issue of creativity and my concern for the noticeable and gradual abandonment of art therapy as an important component of psychiatric healing therapy. Over the past few decades, the prominence and ease of prescribing medication therapy seems to have overshadowed other non-medication therapies, including art therapy. Added to that, the frequent budgetary constraints in mental health funding, compounded by the significant rise in the cost of new psychiatric medications has left little for other therapies. Though the lack of funding is a serious enough reason for the decline in interest and the application of art therapy and other psychosocial approaches, I believe a number of other important issues have contributed to this noticeable decline. A lack of serious champions for the full implementation of the biopsychosocial model has denied the field a strong advocacy, on the face of a much stronger advocacy and support from the pharmaceutical sectors. As expected, the decline in the funding of non-medication therapies has managed to make such therapies less visible and has reduced the availability, unless one can afford to pay for it privately, which is not an affordable option for many psychiatric patients who are struggling with major psychiatric disorders.

As a circular phenomenon, the lack of funding, low visibility and decreased advocacy has resulted in the decline of research interest in this important field, making it harder to obtain funding for research. A comprehensive lack of interest has been gradually occurring, in spite of the positive data from surveys that indicate the high value of complementary non-medication therapies that are rated favourably by patients, contributing to their own healing and recovery, and who add comments such as, "...(art therapy) has significantly helped me with better integration..." and "...it allowed me to be able to express myself, when words were difficult to find...", and so on. Hardly any other field of psychiatric therapy can garner such an enthusiastic endorsement. Though the application of art therapy in general psychiatric practice has been in a state of decline, the science of creativity, a related concept, seems to attract a good deal of neuroscience research interest and, in particular, its relationship to emotions and psychiatric disorders.

For a long time, designations such as "mad artist", "mad choreographer" or "mad genius", among many others, has been popularized by the many publications and documentaries linking creativity to emotions and, in some cases, psychiatric disorders. Yet, the majority of surveys conducted in recent decades has failed to confirm such a relationship. A long list of celebrities and big names who have been treated for some form of psychiatric difficulty or diagnosed with a recognized psychiatric disorder, has continued to be used as evidence of this relationship. Inevitably, such a quandary begs the question of whether creative individuals are more likely to be vulnerable to emotional issues, or formally suffer from a recognized psychiatric disorder. Alternatively, the issue can be re-framed to pose the question of whether persons suffering from psychiatric disorders are more likely to be more creative than the average non-clinical population. Unfortunately, in spite of the recent interest and research efforts, the current extensive literature cannot provide a clear or definitive statement, one way or another. Even with the introduction of the more precise neuroimaging technologies that have opened a window on the inner workings of the brain, creativity as a neuroscience concept continues to be challenged and compromised by several methodological limitations.

As a concept, creativity is too broad to be reliably defined. It is not surprising, then, the many definitions that already exist. An Encyclopedia Britannica definition describes creativity as "the ability to make or bring into existence something new, such as a new solution to a problem, a new method, a new device, or a new artistic object or form". Another definition offered by author Robert E. Franklin, in his book manuscript "Human Motivation", defines creativity as "the tendency to generate or recognize ideas, alternatives, or possibilities that may be useful in solving problems, communicating with others, and entertaining ourselves and others". The writer and film maker Kelly Morr (Twitter@KelMo), defines creativity as the ability to transcend traditional ways of thinking or acting, and to develop new and original ideas, methods or objects". One can go and on, without finding a clear definition that encompasses all of its components and is also practical enough to inform and measure. At present, we are unable to find an agreement on one definition. Maybe it is not even realistic to expect an all-encompassing definition.

In that case, it may be more practical and informative to breakdown the concept into manageable smaller components that, conceptually, are believed to be contributors to the concept. For example, there already exists some evidence to implicate cognitive abilities, intelligence and mood states. For now, at a minimum, researchers in this field, particularly those planning expensive neuroimaging studies, should include clearly in their manuscripts a definition of creativity as it is applied in their study. Another challenge is to ensure the reliability and validity of measurement tools that are, to a large extent, dependent on the orientation and the conceptual model that is capable of underpinning the issues behind the concept. My purpose is not to slow the research process in creativity, but to make it more reliable and its conclusions more consistent and replicable.

In the end, the germane question is whether the neuroscience of creativity matters among the many other pressing neuroscience challenges. I do believe that the study of creativity is important and does matter. To begin with, there exists a number of reasonable theories that evolutionally link the development of creativity to adaptation and better survival. Creativity is limitless and can add and improve whatever anyone is doing in the course of our daily life. It is enriching and conveys a level of meaning and mental satisfaction. It strengthens self-concept and ensures a positive role in life. Collectively, creativity enhances the contribution of individuals in the advancement of their communities and its progress. Creativity is not just an innate attribute, it can be acquired or improved. It is a contributor to a better mental health state. For those members of the society who, unfortunately, may get hit with one of the major psychiatric disorders, such as schizophrenia or persistent severe depression, clarifying the neuroscience of creativity assumes more significance.

Though the current neuroscience of creativity is still in its infancy and far from being definitive, available data indicates that the brain areas involved in creativity are close to those areas that appear to be involved in emotions and imaginative thinking. The imaginative network seems to involve communication within the frontal cortex and within the parietal lobe. Though such early and tentative assumptions are still a work in progress, one is tempted to wonder about the close proximity of these areas in the brain and to speculate whether the imaginative network, being close to the thinking and emotions region, may be behind the detailed richness of abnormal thoughts frequently encountered in a number of psychiatric disorders. It's just a speculation, or rather, imaginatively thinking aloud.

Loneliness: The Invisible and Silent Disorder

**"...What I need most is to have a friend to go out
with from time to time, to have coffee."**

- A patient attending a psychosis clinic

Certainly, the above quote is a clear statement by a patient attending an outpatient clinic for treatment of schizophrenic and psychotic disorders, in response to a survey among attendants of the clinic. Patients were asked to list the top ten priorities and needs that require more attention. Surprisingly, feelings of loneliness and isolation topped the list, displacing what we thought would be the top concerns, such as medications and their side effects; a frequently raised concern. On the other hand, thinking about the life of a person who is quite often struggling with psychotic experiences, the choice of loneliness at the top of emerging gaps and needs should not be that surprising. Not only do patients struggle with multiple limitations, such as fear, stigma, concerns about being judged or not making sense to others, but also by the limitations related to living in a distorted personal world that at times can be confusing and frightening, all driven by a shaken sense of reality. I have to admit, though the results of the survey were not what we expected, what we heard from patients proved serious enough to add the issue of loneliness to our research agenda for patient-centred care. It also elevated the importance of the subject of loneliness to be included on the list of challenges discussed in this book. But, before I go further in detailing what we already know about the medical and psychiatric impact of loneliness, one has to define what loneliness is and what it is not.

As an important concept, there exists several definitions of loneliness that are frequently based on the professional or scientific orientation of the researcher or the speaker. Quite often, loneliness is defined by its impact. An example of this approach defines loneliness as a universal human experience, yet it is unique for the individual and can lead to distress and depression. Other definitions approach loneliness as conceptually being the gap or discrepancy between the individual's desire and their achieved levels of social engagement. The wider the gap, the greater the loneliness. Another approach has been simply to define loneliness as the experience of emotional and social isolation, as clearly expressed by the patient.

One of the most interesting and gratifying aspects of having worked closely with patients, has been the mutual trust in the therapeutic relationship that frequently included me in their very private emotional space. As a manifestation of such trust, the following expression by one of my patients attempts to describe in prose what she felt about loneliness, and who shared it with me. It was written after attending a long-term clinic, after conquering loneliness following a social engagement intervention. It is an elegant attempt to define the feeling of loneliness.

"Loneliness"
It is not just being alone
It is emotionless.
It is a vacuum or empty space,
It feels like a void,
Painful, feeling isolated and lost,
It is a powerful dark screen
That shuts the light off.
It is feeling hopeless and being depressed,
Unable nor wanting to reach out.
It is simply a soul being lost,
The mind is empty, missing joy and thrust.

My own preference for a definition describes loneliness as not necessarily being alone, but as the perception of being alone and isolated. Yet, in spite of the wide range of proposed definitions, there exists a common agreement that loneliness can be experienced even when one is in a crowd. Being alone is not to be equated with loneliness. Historically, and up to the present time, isolation can be part of a religious solitude practice or cultural ritual, self-chosen as a fulfillment of spiritual orthodoxy. Another agreed upon common feature of loneliness is being uniquely individual and a subjective experience. This is where I have a number of critical research comments regarding the design of several of the reported research studies of the concept of loneliness, particularly in recent neuroimaging studies that have attempted to explore the psychobiology and neurobiology of loneliness.

But, before I share my critical comments, let me briefly summarize what is known about the neurobiology of loneliness, which is in its early infancy. So far, most of the available data seems to be inconsistent and often lacks a coherent conceptual framework that connects the disparate focal dots in the brain. Data about brain mapping covers a broad area, ranging from the prefrontal cortex, the amygdala and the limbic striatum. Interestingly enough, these areas of the brain that are assumed to be involved in the regulation of social behaviour are also involved in pain perception and emotional processing.

Similarly, the molecular biology data continues to be unclear, pointing to a role for oxytocin, the hormone known as the "hormone of calm" and social regulation. More recently, the neurotransmitter serotonin, which is supposed to play a major role in depression, has also been implicated in the regulation of social behaviour. Of late, endorphins have been demonstrated in animals to have a role in physical contact, such as when grooming, and has also been implicated in human behaviour during conjoint activities, such as dancing or group singing.

Overall, there is an acceptance of the early efforts to bridge the divide between loneliness as a social construct and its relation to certain brain neural networks or regional brain functioning. However, it is clear that such research efforts are in their very early phase. That also means that future studies, particularly the complex and expensive neuroimaging studies, ought to be rigorously designed. And here, once more, are my critical comments, after reviewing several published reports. The central concern being that loneliness as a subjective construct, requires proof of the concept before launching into the exploration of its neurobiology. Any reasonable proof of a subjective concept, as detailed in my 2021 book, requires a few important elements. The concept and ad priori has to be defined as being used in the particular study. The tools for assessment and measurement of loneliness have to be of proven reliability and validity. Similarly, as a subjective self-reported state, reliability of patients to consistently and reliably report their inner feelings has to be demonstrated. Any research approach or design must be developed based on a hypothesized conceptual framework. Not adhering to such requirements can cast doubt on any results. It is much better to approach the study design on solid grounds, right from the beginning.

The Medical and Psychiatric Implications of Loneliness

As loneliness is a universal human concept, there exists significant literature both in the humanities and medicine, ranging from sentimental poems, sad folk songs and heartbreaking novels, to an extensive and evolving literature about its personal, medical and psychiatric impact. As mentioned previously, the World Health Organization has already declared loneliness a health risk worldwide. The physiological and immunological human impact are well-documented, in terms of pulse, blood pressure, heart rate and other important autonomic functions, as well as lowered immunity in general. It worsens disease processes, complicating treatment course and outcome in a similar pattern to what we see in response to sustained situations of stress.

Psychiatric patients, by the very nature of their psychiatric afflictions, seem to be more vulnerable to the debilitating impact of loneliness that includes anxiety, depression, self-harm notions and low self-image and self-concept. The absence of rewarding social contact that can trigger the dopamine reaction, can easily lead to alcohol use and abuse. Additionally, disrupted sleep patterns and a lack of physical activity included with social interactions, can make the physical and mental impact of loneliness much more pronounced. Dissatisfaction, impaired quality of life and quality of living, are generally the expected outcomes, as disabilities become more detrimental. With aging, the elderly population can be seriously impacted and the aging process becomes deleterious, not just physically and socially, but economically too, as often noted in situations of disabilities resulting from advanced dementia, as in Alzheimer's. It is interesting that some recent studies have identified early signs of loneliness as an early marker for the development of Alzheimer's dementia, which was correlated with the appearance of amyloid patches in the brain.

In essence, evidence already exists and points clearly to increased morbidity and mortality related to loneliness in medical and non-medical populations. It is a major public health challenge, not only in its medical or psychiatric dimensions, but more so in economic and life planning, particularly for the rapidly increasing number of elderly patients. Such major challenges have to be met by optimal health and economic planning. It requires adequate contributions from a vast field of experts, including health scientists, neuroscientists, population health scientists, epidemiologists, sociologists, economists and even from designers and architects. It is a real challenge for a real need, that has been waiting for human approaches with science and expertise at its core.

The Fear of Taking Medications - The Nocebo Concept

"...The best medications are of no value unless they are taken."

- A. G. Awad 2019

One weekend in February 2022, while composing this chapter, I felt bombarded by various electronic media, in their reports of the loud and extensive protests of the anti-vaccine demonstrators marching in most big cities. The fervour, anger and veracity of some of the demonstrators betrayed what is going on over weeks of campaigning broad misinformation and disinformation of how vaccines have become more of a political issue than a simple medical one. On the other hand, I believe that many physicians, during the course of their clinical practice have encountered several patients to get the vaccine, outside of any conspiracy circles, who genuinely and truly felt fearful of taking medication, including vaccines.

The origins of such experienced or imagined fears are certainly multiple, but the inclusion of the less than candid advertisement of medications and their side effects by the pharmaceutical industry, in print or various electronic media, might be one reason for the resistance. Frequently, such brief advertisements are felt to be deceptive, initially touting the many benefits of the medication, and at the very tail end of the commercial that lasts no more than 30-40 seconds, a brief and quick warning about several potential and serious side effects is delivered. It is not possible in the 30-40 seconds it takes to deliver a detailed and balanced account, but leaving the warning about serious side effects to the last few seconds, tends to leave the viewers feeling suspicious about the likely hidden agenda. What viewers then can do, is go to other media in search of more information that would likely not be free of other biases. In the end, fear of medications becomes consolidated in the minds of many viewers. The dilemma for physicians is a double-edged sword. On one hand, the physician has the obligation to fully disclose all the pros and cons of the medication or any other recommended therapeutic intervention, and on the other hand, physicians have to skilfully undo the preconceived fears and suspicions. It is certainly a delicate and challenging task.

The fear of taking medications is certainly a complex process that has many aspects to it. Unfortunately, such a phenomenon, given the name "nocebo response", has not received as much research interest similar to that given to its opposite, the "placebo response". Both the nocebo and the placebo responses are the opposite sides of the same coin. Indeed, the nocebo response is frequently described as the "evil twin" of the placebo response which is meant to "please". The nocebo term is originally a Latin word meaning "to harm". As the opposite of the placebo effect, the nocebo response defines the negative outcome that occurs, due to the belief that the medication or the intervention would cause some harm. As such, the nocebo is certainly an important medical concept that, unfortunately, has not garnered much research interest until recently. In recent years, there seems to be a revival of research interest related to the rapid development of a vast array of medications and the ongoing effort to enhance outcomes, including the focused and important attention to improving compliant behaviour when it comes to medication.

It is interesting to note that the recent data compiled from several clinical studies of the Covid-19 vaccine reveals that the nocebo effect accounts for about 76%, on average, of all reported adverse reactions to a dose of the vaccine. Similarly, a recent British vast and well-designed clinical study regarding the use of statins, a wide class of medication for lowering cholesterol levels, has found that no more than 10% of users had experienced genuine side-effects of the medication. This new data certainly provides a real challenge to the long-time held medical view of the widespread side effects of the statin class of medications. This data also seems to restore some public health confidence in the use of the reasonably priced and cheaper statins to combat widespread cardiovascular problems in the community, particularly in less affluent societies. Such new and interesting data compels one to ask the same question that I asked regarding the placebo response in my 2021 book: Are there any particular characteristics for those patients with a nocebo response that would make them more vulnerable to respond in such a pattern?

Unfortunately, nothing specific or consistent has been found to characterize the nocebo response, but general trends, such as anxiety, obsessive compulsive tendencies and previous experience with medication can contribute to its undesirable genesis. Quite often it is a simple issue of human nature that contributes to the development of a rather strong belief system. I'm reminded of an old psychological approach called "gaslighting", which has proven to be influential in assimilating false and misleading information into one's own beliefs and convictions. Continually repeating the false information over and over, ends in becoming believable to the point that it can trigger actionable behavioural responses, a process not dissimilar to brainwashing.

It brings to mind an anecdote I encountered in Moscow, where I did part of my post-graduate research studies in the early 1960s. The story was said to be based on true facts that were inherent to the Soviet system at that time, specifically, the common and frequent shortages encountered in several food items. The story goes as follows: A man stood in the main street and, as a joke, started shouting that the food store down the road had received a new shipment of cheap meat, which, as usual, triggered people running to queue in front of the store. After a while, seeing the many people who had already lined up, the man had second thoughts, wondering if maybe it was true, and in turn, he also rushed to join the queue. The moral of the story is that even if it seems to be a fictional parable, it proves the reality of the human condition and how people are susceptible to incorporating misinformation into their belief system. In any case, the construct of the nocebo response is psychiatrically important, as statistical information clearly points out, the result is a relatively low rate of compliance behaviour with medications, particularly among those who are inflicted with major psychiatric problems, such as schizophrenia or severe bipolar depression and are often in need of relying on medications almost indefinitely.

What can be done? This is an important, but difficult question, requiring serious changes in both physicians' attitudes and pharmaceutical industry approaches in the marketing of medications. Efforts are needed to continuously correct misinformation before it is consolidated as a believable fact. A strong therapeutic relationship between the provider and receiver of care can add an important layer of mutual trust and respect for medical recommendations. Transparency in pharmaceutical promotion and marketing can help to restore badly needed trust, as well as a transparent relationship.

The science of the nocebo has to be much better understood. With all of what we know about the placebo response, the good twin of the nocebo, we can improve the development and use of medication for the major purpose of improving psychiatric outcomes and containing costs. Not an easy task.

Prolonging Illness Behaviour and the Contribution of Ruminative and Clinging Behaviours

Before I reflect on the complex behaviour that is the subject matter of this chapter, I feel it is important to first make clear what I mean by "ruminating", "clinging" and define what is meant by "illness behaviour". Though there exists several definitions for the state of rumination, in general most of them agree on its central core, which is the immersive and repetitive negative thinking, which is different from thought searching or emotional processing. It is clear that significant ruminative states can impact negatively on several aspects of cognitive and attentional abilities. It is frequently linked to anxiety and depressive states, but can occur in the context of other psychiatric disorders. In its serious form, excessive ruminative states can be distractive and emotionally depleting by magnifying the impact of stress, which is often implicated in the origin of ruminative thoughts.

Ruminations can be of a reflective, analytical and problem solving pattern, or can be a self-perpetuating type of pattern. Though several theories have been introduced to formulate the psychological origin of such behaviour, the two main and largely overlapping psychological concepts behind the ruminative state include the "response style" theory and the "goal progress" theory. The response style theory defines ruminations as passive repetitive thoughts about the cause and the consequence of one's own distress in general. It is an attempt to cope with self-discrepancy and the gap between the desired and what is achieved. The goal progress theory suggests that individuals are more likely to remember important, but unfinished tasks, rather than those that are already accomplished. It describes the tendency to think recurrently about central, high priority goals that have not yet been attained.

Both theories in general agree on the affective, cognitive and attentional consequences of uncontrolled ruminative states. The neuroscience behind such distracting ruminative behaviour continues to be unclear and not well defined, however, so far most data points to a significant role of the pre-frontal region of the brain. Clinging, on the other hand, is an adjective of ancient Germanic and Dutch origin, that describes a person who adheres and sticks persistently or stubbornly to an object or a thought. It is not difficult, then, to wonder whether clinging is a serious component of the overall ruminative complex experience.

Why then, you might wonder, am I suddenly concerned with the topic and devoting a separate chapter in this book, dealing with the clinical observations. In reality, it is not a sudden idea, as such issues have been with me for some time, as I will explain later. I do believe that many psychiatrists tend to ignore or pay little attention to clinging ruminative behaviour and its relevance to perpetuating and prolonging illness behaviour. However, the most recent reason that vividly reminded me of this challenging behaviour has been reading a book review, published in the New York Times Book Review of January 2022. The book under review is titled, "The Zen of Therapy: Uncovering a Hidden Kindness in Life", authored by the well-known psychiatrist and psychotherapist Mark Epstein. The excellent review was written by Oliver Burkeman, under the interesting title "Of Two Minds", which added more to my curiosity. And that is where the word "clinging" caught my attention and has lingered in my mind for a long time since.

In his book, Mark Epstein, who is a practising Buddhist, attempted to chart a clear course between two approaches in therapy. The one traditional and most practiced clinical approach is attaching a high value to the personal stories that our patients share with us, and the other, a distinctly Buddhist approach, attaches less value and importance to such personal stories. In Buddhism, freedom lies not in understanding what happened to us personally, but in loosening our grip on it all. In other words, to abandon the clinging and fixation of the past or of certain ideas, and to move forward with new goals. And that was the reason that the concept of clinging and the tacit advice to loosen the connection to the past appeared to me as the most attractive concept, contrary to how we, psychiatrists, are generally trained to deeply delve into the past. Though I always felt that the past was only important in developing a sketch of the forces that shaped the development of the person sitting in front of me in therapy, it is of more value to move quickly and not cling to the past for long. It is better to quickly open a path for the future. After all, most of the events of the past, in the end, are "water under the bridge". I am sure that many psychiatrists, particularly those who are in some way still clinging to the waning psychoanalytic orientation, will likely disagree with this opinion. However, leaving such deeply ingrained ideologies aside, there is another important aspect of clinging to the past, which is the prolongation of "illness behaviour". And that was the main reason for writing this chapter, rather than attempting to change ideological minds.

What, then, is "illness behaviour"? I have to admit that illness behaviour is one of the topics that has interested me for a long time, and have frequently written about. Illness behaviour is defined as the cluster of symptoms that the patient has experienced and described, but has no detectable physical origin, which is somewhat similar to conversion dissociative behaviour. I have to admit that this commonly used definition has a major flaw, which is that "absence" of evidence is not equal to "no evidence". More concerning, with relation to this definition, is that almost all psychiatric disorders we have diagnosed so far would qualify, according to such a definition as being illness behaviour rather than a genuine brain disorder. It is a quandary not only in terms, but in substance, since illness behaviour is real and does exist. It is costly in monetary terms that include extensive testing and the ensuing disability support. But, equally important, is its serious emotional cost and the endless suffering it causes, until we fully understand the determinants of illness behaviour and are able to avoid states that perpetuate and prolong this suffering, such as "clinging" to the negative and painful past.

As I noted earlier, being a psychiatric consultant for many years has given me a good view of the various practices and the kind of clinical situations that frequently end in a lack of adequate response to therapy, whether it includes medications, psychotherapy or both. And here is one of the frequent missed or underestimated clinical observations; neglecting to seriously deal with a ruminative, clinging personality structure and behaviour that is accommodated by the persistent delving into the past by psychotherapists. There may be several tools that exist to loosen the clinging of thoughts, and prominent among them are the various shades and grades of mindfulness, enhanced by cognitive restructuring. In the end, I have to admit that I am a fan of Mark Epstein and his ideas for reforming the psychotherapy of the future, by creating more hopeful and manageable future pathways.

The Past is Coming Back as the Future: The Rise, Fall and Rise Again of Psychedelics

Though the term "psychedelic" has a recent history, its original roots are ancient. The use of mind altering substances, mostly of plant origin such as brown mushroom or peyote, goes back to early tribal history, as part of mystical, tribal or religious ritual. Psychedelics have also been used extensively by shamanic healers, as part of folk medicine.

On the other hand, the modern history of psychedelics seems to be relatively recent. It is likely to have started in 1938, following the synthesis of LSD (d-Lysergic acid diethylamide) by the Swiss chemist Albert Hoffman. It was widely reported that he accidentally tried it himself, then issued an interesting report about his experience of taking a tiny dose of LSD. He described its potent hallucinogenic properties and its mind altering impact on levels of consciousness as being in a dream-like state. Such powerful effects quickly attracted the attention of many curious researchers and clinicians. In one account, over one thousand publications were reported to be in print by the year 1960, in what was noted at that time as a major scientific rush, touting its potential for use in medicine and psychiatry. Interestingly enough, a similar scientific rush has been noted in recent years, following the rise again of scientific interest in the field of psychedelics.

In recent history, the term "psychedelic" was first mentioned in 1957, in a correspondence between the British psychiatrist and drug expert Dr. Humphry Osmond and the famous writer, philosopher and futurist Aldous Huxley, who was interested in the field of consciousness and its alteration, and who earlier requested a dose of LSD for self experimentation. Dr. Humphry Osmond was a British-trained psychiatrist who maintained an interest in psychotic and hallucinatory states. In 1951, Dr. Osmond was recruited for a clinical position at the large and antiquated Wayburn Psychiatric Hospital in the province of Saskatchewan, Canada. Within a short time he became the superintendent of the hospital, which came with high authority that allowed him to immerse himself in hallucinogen research, focusing initially on LSD. He eventually teamed up with the then young psychiatrist, Dr. Abram Hoffer, a partnership that lasted for years and, by all accounts, seemed to influence several aspects of the future development of psychiatry in Canada. Both Drs. Osmond and Hoffer were skilfully able to introduce their concept of how mind altering substances, such as LSD, could be of great help in psychiatry. They popularized the idea that hallucinogens could resolve the serious challenges of overcrowding in psychiatric hospitals, which were in a precarious situation at that time, lacking adequate knowledge and treatment of many mental disorders.

One has to imagine the state of psychiatric hospitals in the 1950s, to have an understanding of how new, yet unproven approaches, such as the use of hallucinogens, could quickly gain followers and enthusiasts. The successful introduction of the new antipsychotic Chlorpromazine, and its mostly positive impact, seems to have facilitated the public acceptance of psychoactive substances for use in psychiatric practice. Meanwhile, a change in the Saskatchewan provincial government introduced the New Democratic Party, headed by Premier Tommy Douglas, the first socialist politician to assume such a role in Canada. One of the priorities for the new government was to introduce a national agenda for universal healthcare, which took years of intense politics to eventually materialize in the early 1960s. As part of that push, the government added significant funding for healthcare research, which included significant funding for the Osmond/Hoffer research programs. The enhanced funding managed to introduce new health policies that seemed to create a new culture of research and experimentation. That meant that the province of Saskatchewan became the hub for psychiatric research and, specifically, for psychedelic research that extended to LSD and other substances such as Mescaline, for the treatment of schizophrenia and addictive states.

As happens in situations of extreme but scientifically unfounded hype, the psychedelics failed to deliver the promised "psychiatric revolution", but not before the widely popular use of psychedelics became uncontrollable. The spread of extensive drug sub-culture groups merged with the drug scene of the 1960s and 1970s, pushing the government to put into place restrictions on drug use, which stopped the advocacy and funding of the Osmond/Hoffer psychedelic research programs. Dr. Osmond moved to Princeton University, and Dr. Hoffer shifted his research program to schizophrenia.

Dr. Hoffer's early unorthodox approach, such as the use of mega-vitamins for the treatment of schizophrenia, created controversy within mainstream psychiatry. His dogged fight, with unproven evidence and the unconvincing effectiveness of mega-vitamins in schizophrenia, eventually earned Dr. Hoffer the reputation of being a "hard headed" researcher. As frequently happens in such controversies, the truth could be found somewhere in the middle. True, he was a fierce defender of his concepts and views, but his vision for the development of psychiatric research in Canada yielded several positive results. He was able to attract and recruit several bright, young clinicians and scientists, as his research programs became the training ground for many aspiring young researchers who later became leaders in the psychiatric field in Canada. I believe that in spite of his dogged and sometimes rigid research approach, Professor Hoffer has left several prominent contributions, such as the development of the Canadian Society of Schizophrenia Research in Canada, which he supported as its president for a number of years. Another of his major contributions is the development of the field of orthomolecular psychiatry.

Although I had been in contact with Professor Hoffer a few times, in my capacity as the President of the Canadian College of Neuropsychopharmacology, pertaining to matters related to the business of this college, I met him only once at a private dinner, on the occasion of his retirement. He was truly a charismatic personality who never shied away from controversy. Yet, he managed to save his reputation and career in the end, by leaving the scene of psychedelic research before its implosion by the disclosure of widespread stories of abuse. As it happens, the CIA funded the surreptitious and secret use of hallucinogens for brainwashing experiments, in conjunction with a few academic psychiatric departments in Canada, that led to litigation and the establishment of a commission of inquiry.

Though the collapse of the Osmond/Hoffer programs signalled the end of the formal support and acceptance of research in the hallucinogens field, scientific interest in the field was privately continued by several scientists and clinicians, in pursuit of its potential use in medicine and psychiatry. Using other methods, the rising number of treatment failures, particularly in severe and intractable depression, and heightened media reports over the past few decades, has managed to garner focused research attention once more on psychedelics. Several patient groups seemed to gain an unusual momentum by coalescing together with other medical groups, in putting pressure on government agencies to allow for a formal return of hallucinogens in clinical trials. This time, the pressure was backed and better coordinated by the private sector joining the effort for government to allow a second look at the potential role of psychedelics in offering help for treatment-resistant psychiatric conditions. The rising notion that psychedelics could be helpful in the treatment of post traumatic stress disorder, a diagnosis that had been spreading, particularly in the veteran populations, brought about unlikely veteran organizations to join in the effort to bring back a more focused exploration of the potential benefits of using hallucinogens.

Eventually, a major and well coordinated coalition of patients, tech companies and the private sector managed to get government approval for limited clinical trials of psychedelics in psychiatric disorders, using Ketamine, an NMDA receptor antagonist, to be the first as a trial medication. Ketamine has been around for a long time in Canada, approved as a general anaesthetic. Separately, and unrelated to anaesthesia, in view of its powerful analgesic properties, Ketamine was widely used during the Vietnam War, being included in all medical emergency kits carried by army personnel for use in severe injuries. Ketamine was never approved for a pain indication role, nor for status epileptics, where it was at times used. It is considered to be safe in low doses, but poses several risks in higher doses. Ketamine can produce prolonged dissociative states, sedation and short term memory loss, that earned it the street name of being the "date rape" drug. Like LSD, Ketamine can produce visual and auditory hallucinations, and a sense of detachment from oneself and the surrounding environment, including an ability for memory manipulation. It managed to attract attention for recreational use, as well as a medication for serious cases of post-traumatic stress. This last example was certainly among the reasons for the intense backing and lobbying by veteran groups.

In March 2019, the Food and Drug Administration (FDA) in the US expedited the approval of Esketamine, a derivative of Ketamine, as the first new medication for severe depression, outside the conventional list. Esketamine was to be used for major depression that did not respond to adequate conventional treatments, particularly in emergency situations of serious and impending suicidal intent. Though the approval did not include any information about how Ketamine works pharmacologically in depression, nor was there any information about its long term use, the approval was a landmark decision, in that it opened up the regulatory doors for clinical trials with other hallucinogenic substances. As expected, in no time after the introduction of Esketamine, several private Ketamine clinics suddenly appeared. It is a rather worrisome situation, not only due to the high cost levied for such treatment, but also whether the required standards of care are observed and the collection of accurate clinical information. Regarding private and commercial health entities, my concern has always been that the line between science and commercialism can get easily blurred over time. They require the establishment of close long term monitoring and evaluation of long term use. Nevertheless, the approval of Ketamine in such limited indications is a step forward in opening the door for development of new treatment approaches outside the conventional boxes. Now that NMDA-enabled therapy is rapidly spreading, this development raises serious concerns about the adequate training of therapists and the adherence to a standardized competent process.

Unfortunately, the history of psychiatry is replete with well-intentioned efforts to introduce innovative treatment or diagnostic approaches that become widespread, but ultimately lead to major disappointments and setbacks. From the red spots detected in urine as a marker of schizophrenia, which eventually was discovered to be the residue of the type of tea served to patients in mental asylums, to varieties of a long list of herbal and vitamin remedies, to endless unusual psychotherapy interventions, one has to be careful and humble before spreading unfounded or unproven notions as therapeutic tools. In all such issues, the serious role of regulatory agencies is extremely important and should not be subject to political, commercial or any other sources of influence. It is clear by now, the recent successful rise in interest of the use of psychedelics is just the beginning, and is likely to soon include psilocybin, which is being backed by extensive interest groups and a powerful lobby. However, such major developments have to be closely followed by adequate monitoring and the collection of reliable long term data. Hopefully, the field has already learned enough from past errors, as well as unhelpful and harmful experiences.

Alternative Medicine Versus Alternative "To" Medicine - Reflections on the Blurry Line Between Science and Commercialism

A few years ago, Professor Wagiuh Ishak, with the University of California at Los Angeles, kindly invited me to contribute a chapter to his book "The Handbook of Wellness Medicine", which I enthusiastically fulfilled. The book, which proved to be a most informative and broadly inclusive text book about wellness medicine, was published in 2020 by Cambridge University Press. It included fifty chapters contributed by a long list of experts who covered the field of wellness, from its conceptual models, measurements and applications, to various clinical disciplines and topics, including my chapter, "The Concept of Wellness in Psychiatric and Substance Use Disorders". Being a subjective state, wellness has been one of my major academic interests, along with other issues such as quality of life, satisfaction and preferences, all clinical states that are central to the concept of patient-centred care.

In preparation for my chapter contribution to Professor Ishak's book, I thoroughly searched the most recent literature on wellness, which proved to be overwhelmingly extensive. To my surprise, the majority of available literature was generally of a commercial nature, covering a broad range of promotional material that was lacking in real science. There were many contributors with diverse products and promotional material that included strawberry wellness jams, wellness drinks and diets, wellness jump suits, various exercises, wellness walking shoes, and the list goes on and on. Diverse claims about the products were recommended and backed by highly positive anecdotes or personal testimonials, but rarely with any rigorous science. In no time, I found myself getting lost among the many fantastic and mostly unsupported claims by celebrities and professional promoters, some of whom had a science background.

The conclusion I was left with is that the line between commercialism and science has been significantly blurred. Meaning that, for the average reader, it is difficult or even impossible to ascertain the truth about what is being offered, which includes a broad list of physical, pharmacological, emotional and counselling aids, all marketed as holistic, alternative medicines, or clearly as alternatives "to" medicine. And that is where the confusion and concerns often arise, including mine. Given the phenomenal growth of the wellness industry, in reality it has managed to successfully hijack scientific concepts for the purpose of commercial benefit. There is a pressing need for wellness, but often the outcome of alternative applications are not just frequently ineffective and of little value, but most concerning is the possibility of harm. Giving false hope may delay treatment of a serious condition, or more often there is an unforeseen adverse reaction when an alternative medicinal remedy interacts with other medications, negatively impacting a medical condition.

An interesting personal story of mine that happened few years ago, clearly illustrates the unknown and unexpected clinical impact of using cinnamon, a popular herbal substance that is used in a drink or added to food. In Egypt, where I was born and spent my early years, a popular winter drink was a boiled concoction of cinnamon and ginger. It was offered in coffee shops, not only as an enjoyable drink, but also for its immunological medicinal benefits for protection from flu-like symptoms. I continued to use it frequently as a refreshing warm drink and at times as an alternative to tea or coffee, up until recently. Cinnamon bark and cinnamon powder are usually available in many food stores.

A few years ago, I happened to be shopping at a Chinese food store and purchased some cinnamon. I was struck by how much cheaper it was there, compared to where I usually shopped, but the cinnamon tasted the same. A while later, on Xmas morning, I woke up and suddenly developed a nose bleed that would not stop by pressing or even packing my nose. As my wife was helping to control the bleeding, she asked whether I had taken any medications the evening before. I had taken a low dose of aspirin, and I recalled drinking a cup of the strong cinnamon and ginger drink, with the cinnamon I had bought at the Chinese shop. A quick search of the chemical properties of cinnamon, revealed new and surprising facts that I never knew throughout my many years of medical practice.

For the first time, I learned that there are several varieties of cinnamon, grouped by origin of place. As it turns out, one of the two main varieties is from Sri Lanka and India, and the other one is from China, each with their own somewhat different pharmacological properties. The Chinese variety is cheaper and has a high level of coumarin, a potent blood thinner, compared to the Sri Lankan and Indian variety, which has a lower level of coumarin and is more expensive. Luckily, I had some vitamin K available, which eventually stopped the nose bleeding. Over the following few days, I asked several medical colleagues if they knew about the difference between the Chinese and Indian cinnamon varieties, but no one was aware of the difference, except for the medical colleagues who were from India. Unfortunately, herbal medicine and the potential of drug interactions are not adequately understood nor taught, in spite of their massive popular use. Being of plant origin does not mean it is free of toxic effects. I am not, by any means, calling for the regulation or restriction of herbal medicines, but the illustration of my personal story reveals how important it is to educate physicians about potential benefits and possible harm involved.

Going back to the title of this chapter regarding "alternative medicine" versus "alternative to medicine", the differentiation is important and beyond just a semantic difference. Applying this difference to the concept of wellness, historically is an important concept in medicine that is the ultimate outcome of the successful use of a medical intervention. Over the years, though the concept of wellness was well recognized, it has not received adequate research attention to define what it means in medical practice, nor were adequate concepts developed to provide strong conceptual models of its integration into mainstream clinical approaches. To do so, there needs to be developed an appropriate, reliable and validated methodology for its measurement. It is a clinical process that has no end, but in reality is a continuous process for more improvement and increased feelings of wellness. In that sense, it is clear that it cannot be called an "alternative medicine". In truth, wellness is the means and objective of medicine in any medical or psychiatric intervention.

It is clear that in applying subjective constructs to psychiatry and psychiatric practice, the concept of wellness has to be adapted in a more realistic way to the life of the majority of psychiatric patients suffering from serious psychiatric disorders, such as schizophrenia, dementia and others. It has to be recognized that wellness, in this case, is a life long process that is frequently reevaluated and adapted to the unfortunately long term of major psychiatric afflictions. It is not an alternative to medicine, but possibly at its best can supplement medicine. For that, physicians need to be adequately informed of the subject and have it included in the training curriculum.

Can Physicians Ethically Practice Against Science and Mainstream Medical Consensus?

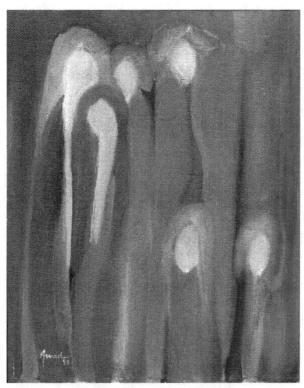

**"Protest. Mothers Protesting Disappearance of Their Sons
in Chile During the Pinochet Dictatorship" 1984**
by the author, A. G. Awad,
Oil on canvas board 20"x 25"

Reading the Canadian national newspaper "The Toronto Star" on June 16, 2022, I found a new report with the title "Anti-vaccine Doctor Sentenced to Prison for Capital Riot". The article was written by Michael Kunzelman for the Associated Press. The report detailed the outcome of the trial of a California physician (name omitted for this book), a leading figure in the US anti-vaccine protest movement, who was sentenced to two months in prison followed by twelve months of supervised release for storming the US capitol and delivering a speech to the rioters. Though the judge declared that the sentencing was based on the offence of breaching capitol security, he also noted that the accused physician was the founder of "America's Frontline Doctors", an activist group known for spreading Covid-19 misinformation, which was what grabbed my attention, and not in any way minimized her reprehensible misconduct and role in the January 6 violent insurrection.

A few days earlier, there was some published local Canadian news about a couple of Canadian physicians being referred to the disciplinary committee of the provincial College of Physicians and Surgeons, being accused of spreading Covid-19 misinformation. At that point, I became interested to learn how wide such protests and Covid-19 misinformation had been spread. Generally, what happens in the US finds its way rapidly across the border and into Canada. Searching the matter, I quickly recognized that the Federation of State Medical Boards in the US has circulated a clear warning that providing misinformation about the Covid-19 vaccine contradicts physicians' ethical and professional responsibilities, making them liable for disciplinary hearings, including the possible revocation of their medical licence.

Though such warnings by the Federation of State Medical Boards are not unusual, it met some criticism in its lack of defining what is meant by "misinformation". In contrast, and much earlier, the College of Physicians and Surgeons of Ontario (Canada) circulated a similar warning to physicians and included a clearer definition, and a statement that it was not intended to stifle a healthy public debate about the best way to address any conflictual aspects in the management of the Covid-19 pandemic. The Ontario College of Physicians and Surgeons added that physicians have a professional responsibility not to communicate anti-vaccine, anti-masking, anti-distancing and anti-lockdown statements, or promote unsupported, unproven treatments for Covid-19. As the pandemic dragged on, frustrations among segments of the population deepened and grew, not only through the influence of social media, but also by the political leadership that managed to convert the issue of vaccine into an entrenched political debate that became entangled in individual civil rights issues.

A number of recent surveys of national and international samples have pointed to a clearly mixed response regarding rates of vaccine acceptance, hesitancy and refusal, particularly among health workers, who are supposed to be champions for vaccines. Several surveys clarified the nature and extent of Covid-19 vaccine hesitancy. One of the recent world wide surveys published in the "Journal of Community Health" in 2021, revealed a wide variance in the rate of hesitancy, ranging from 4.3% to almost 72% of the samples. The authors identified issues related to vaccine safety, efficacy and potential side effects among the reasons behind the high rates of hesitancy. Those most likely to accept the vaccine included males over age 50, as well as physicians. However another recent survey just published in April 20, 2022 in the journal "Vaccine", raises more troubling conclusions. The paper by Timothy Gallaghan et al, has the title "Imperfect Messenger?". An analysis of vaccine confidence among primary care physicians. The results of the survey included a troubling 10% of surveyed primary care physicians lack high levels of vaccine confidence and, accordingly, such a relatively large proportion could not be trusted to adequately promote vaccine. Another recently published paper by Eric Merkley and Peter Loewen in the journal "Vaccine" in March 2022, investigated correlates of the dynamics of Covid-19 vaccine-specific hesitancy. The authors conclude that examining the issue of hesitancy to take vaccines ought not to be based only on its attitudinal and demographic correlates, but also needs to include the characteristics of the vaccine themselves.

Putting this data together, it is clear that several issues related to the use of vaccines continues to be the subject of a conflictual state, which is not new and has been with us as long as vaccines have existed. Physicians, as private citizens, are certainly entitled to their own views or beliefs about vaccines, but when it comes to their clinical practice, it is a different matter. Their clinical practice has to be beyond their own beliefs, and strictly guided by science and the prevailing medical consensus. In other words, physicians have an obligation to discuss the benefits, potential side effects and harm, without interjecting their own values or beliefs. A truly important and serious balancing act that ought to not include physicians' personal views. It does not have to include the spreading of false or unproven theories or treatments. One of the basic tenets of the oath that all physicians undertake is the central concept of "do no harm".

Yet, for some physicians to deliberately spread misinformation, overstepping their oath, it is a grave error of judgment. Lumping vaccine protests with political activism, as in the case of the California doctor who joined the January 6 capitol riots, as described above, is a strong and likely sign of lack of knowledge and misguided analysis of the extensive volume of available data that can better guide physicians' decisions. I do strongly believe that physicians have to be trained on how to read clinical journals and be able to reach a correct synthesis of the data and information included.

To the credit of the late Professor David Sachett, previously from MacMaster University in Hamilton Canada, among his extensive contributions to the Foundation of Clinical Epidemiology and many other important issues, such as evidence based medicine, in the 1980s, Professor Sachett contributed a major series on how to read clinical journals, which was published in the Canadian Medical Association Journal. Such a valuable contribution ought to be on the desk of every physician. It may convince a few of the vaccine-denier physicians that they likely had not correctly read the literature. True, there are still a number of controversies that may continue to be conflictual, but, certainly, patients need not be caught in such unresolved conflicts.

Aging and Its Many Impacts

a) Aging Gracefully. Really?!

My interest in aging and its impacts goes back several decades to the mid-1970s, when I accepted a senior clinical and administrative position at a major psychiatric hospital in Toronto. It is currently the Centre for Addiction and Mental Health (CAMH), but at that time it was named the Queen Street Mental Health Centre, or was simply referred to as "999 Queen Street".

As is customary for new senior appointees, I scheduled a few personal meetings with the Chiefs of all the clinical programs, including a meeting with the Chief of Psychogeriatric Services. The psychogeriatric program at the hospital was the major provincial psychogeriatric facility, which predominantly provided in-hospital psychiatric care to the elderly. The program was crowded and inadequately staffed, which clearly reflected the poor status of psychogeriatrics, at that time. The Chief of the psychogeriatrics program was candid about the many gaps and inadequacies in the provision of psychiatric services to the elderly population, which came with under-funding and a lack of interest among many young psychiatrists in seeking further specialized training in psychogeriatrics. At that time, the leading psychogeriatric programs, both in services and academics, were in the United Kingdom. At our meeting, the Director of the program lamented the lack of adequate programming, in spite of the well known and available statistical information, including the clear future projections of the marked increase in the percentage of the elderly among the population.

That was the beginning of my interest in the process of aging and its impact on the provision of medical and psychiatric care. In a few years, my interest in the organization of psychiatric care in general evolved and became a major focus of my academic interests. One of the major challenges for me, then, was how to enhance the academic and scientific aspects of psychiatric care, which led me, with the support of a few colleagues, to establish an annual symposium that dealt with challenging academic interests that can add a beneficial contribution to clinical management and programming. The idea proved to be a remarkable success, particularly after the first of such symposia, about the "Evaluation of Quality of Care in Psychiatry", held in 1978 and the first of its kind, with its proceedings edited and published in a book of the same title the following year.

By the early 1980s, in response to the public outcry about the inadequacies in the provision of psychiatric care to the elderly, the provincial government had some kind of awakening that led to more enhanced funding. Similarly, academic psychiatric departments faced challenges in creating adequate psychogeriatric training programs that appealed to young psychiatrists to further seek training in this rapidly evolving field, with its established specialized divisions of psychogeriatrics that were developed in almost every major academic centre, including the University of Toronto. This was a major development, not only for training purposes, but also somewhat formalized the relationship between psychiatry and geriatric medicine.

By the mid-1980s, several major psychogeriatric programs were developed across Canada and were mostly modelled on the United Kingdom's approach, which quickly proved to be successful, not only improving psychiatric care for the elderly, but also enhanced interest in training for geriatric psychiatry. With the encouraging progress and growth of clinical geriatric services, clinical challenges became more apparent, as they required appropriate resolutions and new ways of thinking. The use of psychiatric medications in the elderly population is an example of one such issue that was a challenge that managed to elevate concerns, drawing broad criticism in the various media. There were headlines in the national and local media, such as "drugging the elderly" and "misuse and abuse of medications in the elderly", and so on. This was the moment for me and a few of my colleagues who were involved in the planning of the annual academic symposia, to take notice and devote the 1985 annual symposium to the issue of "disturbed behaviour in the elderly". The symposium proved to be timely, bringing together experts from various related fields, who shared their experiences on how to appropriately manage the disturbed elderly and chart future directions. Once more, the following year the proceedings were published by Perganon Press and widely distributed.

The 1985 symposium was a turning point for me, in that I became much more aware and focused on the process of aging and how to deal with its psychiatric and medical consequences. Not surprisingly, at that time there was a distinct increase in the number of publications that focused on various topics related to aging and how to age gracefully. As frequently happens with an interesting and unavoidable prospect that awaits every individual, the topic of aging and how to improve it or delay it was suddenly seized upon by lucrative commercial interests and turned it into a major industry, leading to an obvious blurring of the line between science and commercialism. One of the powerful themes and trends that captured the interest of a large segment of the population, is the issue of how to age gracefully. In recent decades, hundreds of books and other publications have flooded the market, with each one recommending highly prescribed formulas to maintain a youthful appearance or, at least, to make aging a more graceful process.

What, then, does "aging gracefully" mean? Though there is no one definition that captures what it means or involves, a large number of published reports seem to focus on the aspect of appearance, rather than on the substantial emotional, psychological and medical aspects of aging. The sad reality has been that "aging gracefully" seems to be a paradox in terms. The core of aging certainly represents a progressive state of losses; personal, social, medical and economic. I still recall my experience in Rome, Italy in 1968, where I was completing my year of post-doctoral training at the Institute of Health Research. At the end of the year, I announced my acceptance of an academic post in the newly opened School of Medicine at the University of Calgary in Canada. My supervisor, as well as a few other colleagues, seriously advised me to be aware that after working in Canada or the US, elderly people frequently became poor, because the pensions were usually rather low or non-existent, in comparison to European countries. Years later, as I settled in Canada, this concern proved to be true for a large portion of Canadian citizens. The inadequacy of pension plans can make it difficult to maintain aspects of the pre-retirement standard of living. Plus the noted social and gradual erosion through death of family members and friends is a part of the continuous narrowing of the social support network, particularly after the children become independent and pursue their own life and careers, and leaving the family nest empty.

So what, then, does gracefully aging involve? Obviously, a broad concept such as aging is complex, being mostly subjective and uniquely individual-based. It depends on a multitude of factors and circumstances, many of which are often outside of ones personal control. The term "aging gracefully" has a conveyed negative connotation too, being used as a euphemism for looking old, but still somehow holding on. My own concept of aging gracefully, far from being a precise definition, is that of being mostly well preserved cognitively, emotionally, medically and socially, to a reasonable degree that allows for room to function and enjoy a good level of quality of life and quality of living. The reason to qualify such a broad concept is that it is unrealistic to expect the preservation of mental and physical faculties equal to as they were twenty or thirty years earlier.

This is where I have a few critical comments about community educational programs for the elderly and how aging is often presented. As I mentioned earlier, aging is a state of continued losses that people need to recognize much earlier and are able to deal in advance with its potential impact. Aging is far more complex than simply having more free time, or being relieved from the duties of a mundane job after many years. Retirement and aging can certainly have real benefits, but such benefits don't always follow automatically. It requires anticipation, recognition and preparation. Frequently, professional counselling for the elderly includes persistent urging to develop a hobby or enlist in a social club. The reality, sadly, is that it is difficult to develop a new hobby when one has never seriously considered it prior to retiring.

With all of the limitations and concerns about aging, and the multiple pressures and persuasion to age gracefully, how on earth does one cope with the inherent and unavoidable losses? Bearing in mind, also, that by the year 2050, projections indicate the number of those over sixty years of age will be more than those below the age of twenty. As in many popular subjective states, aging, like other subjective states, such as wellness or psychedelic ecstasy, can lend itself to extensive commercial applications that often end in a blurring of the line between real science and commercial claims. Indeed, the commercialization of aging and related topics has already been developed into a major and lucrative industry. How to look younger and how to delay aging or, better yet, stop aging altogether, has been a desired and valued dream for human-beings as far back as humans have existed. Looking back to ancient tribal history, rituals have included all modes of looking younger and stronger. It is no surprise to anyone that the industry of aging, or, more precisely, the industry of how to beat aging and look young, has proven to be lucrative and successful for some time.

In modern times, keen scientists are progressively interested in unlocking the mysteries of aging, but, unfortunately, we are not there yet. Meanwhile, until that happens, it is more practical and potentially attainable to pay equal attention to dealing well with age-related illnesses, such as cardiovascular, metabolic or neuromuscular disorders, etc. Improving one's medical status certainly can be a major element in achieving graceful aging. Equally as practical and attainable, is to focus on the development of appropriate social roles that can lead to meaningful connections and satisfying relationships.

My main purpose in writing this chapter about aging, is first to erect sign posts for the readers to recognize the many issues and challenges behind the concept of aging and beyond all the popular commercial claims. It is not my plan to include an exhaustive manifesto of what to do or not do, in order to achieve graceful and harmonious aging. I will leave that to the many serious publications that continue to flood the market with that theme. Yet, not to leave readers in a state of suspense about what I personally consider to be one of the main ingredients in achieving aging gracefully is "being yourself, not your age", a critical attribute. In other words, being authentic to the way you are and not the way you think you should be.

I'm reminded of an interesting, but sad incident, that clearly touches on the issue of authenticity. Many years back, a senior colleague of mine, both in expertise and also in age, was attending a conference in the US with his wife. He was known as an enthusiastic fan of dancing, and one of his passionate wishes during that trip, was to learn how to do a vigorous new dance known as "the calypso". He managed to learn the dance moves with the help of a pretty, young instructor, following a dinner party. After the dance, his wife humorously commented, "You better behave your age". A few minutes later, sadly, he dropped dead, but not before he got his wish to dance the calypso. Obviously, it was a tragic event, and most likely a sad coincidence. Yet, it demonstrates both sides of behaving authentically, the love of fun and life, and the ability to not be worried about how one is perceived by an audience of colleagues. In essence, he behaved himself as he was, fun loving and truly authentic; a wonderful personality trait, that may explain why he was adored by his many patients and colleagues.

Finally, one of the questions that I frequently have been asked is, "Would physical improvements in appearance, such as the use of botox or a minor cosmetic surgical enhancement increase the chance of aging gracefully? My usual response has been that it might, as being comfortable and satisfied with how we look can add to our self-confidence, provided such enhancements do not make you look like a caricature of yourself.

b) Long Term Care and Family Burden of Caring

One of the glaring gaps and deficiencies in healthcare that was exposed by the Covid-19 pandemic over the last couple of years, was the devastating effect of the Covid-19 virus was much more pronounced in long term healthcare facilities in several countries. The wide and rapid spread of the Covid-19 virus, as well as the rate of death among the residents of many long term care facilities, far exceeded those incidents of infections in the elderly in other types of facilities. In reality, such a sad finding is not that surprising, taking into account the long known public litany regarding the poor quality of care provided in many such facilities, which are mostly privately owned and run. Many of these long term facilities are crowded, frequently employ less qualified staff, and often ignore or fail to fully implement the required standards of care.

Obviously, unacceptable conditions at long term care facilities are not the rule everywhere. There exists a number of facilities of a better quality, but they are mostly unaffordable for a large portion of the elderly population, unless covered by private medical insurance. Concern about the quality of care in many long term facilities is not new, nor has it been limited to the serious public impact of the Covid-19 pandemic. Complaints have been rising over the past few decades, along with a rise in demand on such services, unfortunately. The social, economic and cultural changes over the past fifty years has steadily increased the necessity for these facilities.

The gradual disappearance of the concept of the "extended family", pushed further by significant economic imperatives, has quickly and culturally made it acceptable to place elderly family members who cannot take care of themselves, into such institutional facilities. The absence or low access to home care services makes such a decision inevitable, even with the full knowledge of the possible detrimental effect of such a placement, in terms of social and environmental disruptions and dislocations. It is a vexing issue that presents with several serious aspects to it; economic, social and moral. Governments over time have promised better long term care, but very little has changed. Universal coverage, as in the case of basic healthcare, is mostly unaffordable and presently unobtainable without highly expensive public tax hikes.

At the same time, society has an invested interest in the younger generation of the family to pursue a productive career, but they need help with the care of their elderly members, to continue to be cared for in their own homes. It is a major challenge, then, to develop an effective at-home care program, and to organize and fund the only alternative possible, to avoid institutional care for many of the elderly whose health is declining. It is also a moral imperative for society to take care of their elderly citizens to receive needed care in their homes, and in the environment that they have adapted to. In the end, regardless of the quality of the home care program, some elderly patients will still require placement, but hopefully they will be the minority. However, even in the best case scenario for home care, family involvement in the care of their elderly members would hopefully continue, but with a reduced level of burden.

c) Burden of Caring in Major Psychiatric Disorders

As detailed in my book last year, "The Search For a New Psychiatry", the role of the family in taking care of their family members inflicted with a major psychiatric problem, such as schizophrenia, bipolar mood disorder or dementia, has markedly expanded since the 1950s, following the precipitous discharge of chronic psychiatric patients from the mental asylums to a community that was not prepared or ready to accept them. The families, then, had to accept the role of the major caregiver for their ill family members, a role that formally integrated family care into the overall care plan. Examining the burden of family care in schizophrenia, we conducted a major study that involved over 800 patients with the diagnosis of schizophrenia and over 1300 caregivers, all were followed for about four years.

The results were revealing, in that they documented the high burden of care put on the family, in terms of the emotional and physical impact. The results clearly documented a significant decline in family social life, an increase in family conflicts and disagreements, and the frequent cancellation of vacation plans. In addition to various economic difficulties, caregivers experienced more incidents of depression, anxiety and overall distress, as well as more work days were lost by family members. A significant deterioration of the physical health of the caregiver was noted, as well as more visits to hospital emergency departments or to their family physicians. Overall, the results painted a serious and distressing situation, not only for the principle family caregiver, but it also involved other members of the family. As for the patients, their perception of their treatment and their overall expectations were often in significant discrepancy with those of the family, leading to more conflicts and disagreements.

No doubt, the burden of family care in situations with major psychiatric disorders is significant and stressful, particularly in the case of when the caring parents are elderly and they themselves are in need of some support and help. Indeed, adequate home care support can prove helpful to parents and the family in taking better care of their psychiatrically ill members. It would further support the urgent need to introduce more effective home care programs, reducing reliance on institutional care and keeping the family structure as intact as possible. It would ease the burden for the family, while making it possible to continue their involvement with ill and elderly family members. Overall, aging and how to manage its impact is certainly a complex issue, one that we had better face before it becomes a costly and unresolvable challenge.

POSTSCRIPT IN MEMORIAM

Professor Thomas Arthur Ban
1929 – 2022

Photo of Tom Ban

In early February 2022, when I was at the very end of the manuscript for this book, I was deeply saddened to be informed by Christopher, the son of my close friend Thomas Ban, about his father's death. For a couple of weeks prior, I was periodically updated regarding Tom's grave condition, following a massive stroke. Though there was no encouraging news, I consistently believed and frequently told Christopher that Tom had always been a super resilient person to survive until the age of ninety-three. Unfortunately, my hopes of him recovering were dashed by the extent of brain damage after the stroke.

Tom, as he preferred to be called, was the most genial of friends and the most cultured of human beings, with his love of poetry, music and the arts. He was also a caring humanist, having helped so many through his extensive contribution to science and his genuine scientific curiosity. He was always a keen listener, always compassionate and optimistic. Over the past two-and-a-half years, during the restrictions imposed by the Covid-19 pandemic, our bi-weekly phone encounter, often lasting over an hour at a time, was an event that both of us waited for and filled with valuable recollections and extensive reflections. Though the difference in our age was less than five years, he always mused that I was still young, according to the shared notion that anyone younger than either of us was young. Putting aside both our advanced ages, on the phone his vigour and infectious enthusiasm overshadowed any question related to age.

Until a couple of weeks prior to his stroke we were talking about the future, in the context of the manuscript that I had almost completed for this book, regarding the search for a new psychiatry. His enthusiastic support for the central theme of the book; the application of the science of new informatics as the path to apply, in order to save the future of psychiatry, proved to be reassuring and encouraging for me, noting that both of us had started our medical careers in the 1950s, when the terms robot and computer mostly belonged to science fiction. We mused at times about how both our careers mysteriously brought us to Canada, and the dreadful and aggressive Russian invasion of Hungary in 1956 and the undemocratic Russian invasion of Czechoslovakia in 1968, which were behind our quest to seek freedom in Canada, and how we had expressed our gratefulness by the many contributions both of us had made to Canada. Tom successfully managed to cultivate genuine friendships that crossed all national and international boundaries. It's no wonder, then, the numerous tributes, memorials and fond recollections contributed by many of his colleagues, friends and the many whom he trained nationally and internationally.

I have been most honoured to have known Tom since the 1980s, when we first met at the annual meeting of the American College of Neuropsychopharmacology in San Juan, Puerto Rico. In no time, Tom's fascination of anything historical proved to be highly infectious and mutual, as I shared in some of the video interviews that he organized for a series of personal historical accounts. He made contributions to some of the recent historical books about the development of the science of neuropsychopharmacology and its modern organizations.

Moving to Toronto, after his retirement from his professorial tenure at Vanderbilt University in the US, Tom and I further cemented our friendship by periodically meeting for lunch or by phone during the Covid-19 pandemic restrictions. Though Tom has left an extensive list of scientific contributions that are well recognized and extensively reviewed, in this memoriam I wanted to focus on Tom the person and close friend, whom I deeply miss.

International College Neuropsychopharmacology dinner,
with the Ban's and the Awad's,
Paris, France 2007

PART C

Conclusion

This book is the second of a series titled "The Search for a New Psychiatry", launched in 2021. In other words, this book is a follow-up to last year's book, that reviewed the state of our current modern psychiatry, as told through my personal experiences while becoming an academic psychiatrist and clinical neuroscientist. Interestingly enough, the nearly sixty years of my medical career has somewhat corresponded with the history of modern psychiatry, which began in the 1940s and slowly displaced the psychoanalytic era that had gripped psychiatry for several decades. The waning psychoanalytic dogma was profoundly augmented by the development and introduction of a class of specific antipsychotic medications, such as Chlorpromazine and the new antidepressants Imipramine and Nortriptyline, ushering in a major peak of progress and optimism. They carried forward the field of psychiatry and helped to create the modern scientific roots of psychopharmacology, augmenting both biological and community psychiatry.

Unfortunately, in less than two decades, this peak of advancement merged into an extended period of stagnation and slow progress. The gradual recognition of the limitations of the new classes of psychiatric medications proved not to be fully effective in treating the broad spectrum of psychotic symptoms and persistent severe depression, as well as possessing a wide array of side effects, many of which posed serious medical risks. Additionally, the precipitous discharge of long-term and chronic residents of mental asylums to non-welcoming and ill prepared communities that received them, created chaos and crippled any adequate organization of psychiatric services for years to come. Against this backdrop of serious difficulties, progress in psychiatry proceeded in an uneven pattern, with a few peaks of progression separated by long periods of stagnation.

Overall, progress in psychiatry has been perceived as too slow and inadequate to satisfy patients and their families, as well as burdening psychiatrists with many unmet needs in science and clinical practice. Psychiatrists feel unsupported by strong backing from science and have struggled to serve in a clearly underfunded and fragmented service model. They have to contend with imprecise diagnostic systems, in spite of the extensive search for understanding the etiological psychopathology of major psychiatric disorders, that continue as mostly unknown. It was at this point where I stopped in last year's book, and it is also the point from where I continue in this book, with my eyes open to the future of psychiatry and how to save and secure it.

In December of 2019, the Covid-19 pandemic hit everywhere, creating concern and panic in a society that was not adequately prepared to manage it, in terms of public health and an unavailability of appropriate vaccines that could deal with its high contagion and lethality. Miraculously, by late 2020 and early 2021, a consortium of scientists, including immunologists, medical technologists and informatics technology, managed to rapidly develop a new vaccine based on the application of the evolving science of mRNA technology and the employment of artificial intelligence and big data analytics. It was a major scientific feat, considering that in the past it had taken several years to develop a new vaccine.

This major development in science and medical technology left me wondering whether this new scientific approach could be extended to include the management of other medical challenges, particularly in psychiatry, with the purpose of enhancing our understanding of major psychiatric disorders such as schizophrenia, manic depression and severe, unremitting depression. This is what has given me the idea for this book. In recent years I have been impressed by the success of incorporating information technology in a number of medical specialties, such as medical imaging, ophthalmology and dermatology, as well as evolving in several other specialties, like cardiology, oncology, etc.

Knowing in advance the apprehension and the low level of interest in information technology amongst psychiatrists, and the misguided notion of losing the empathic nature of psychiatric practice, I decided to include basic information of the development of information technology and what it can offer to medicine, including its limits and potential risks. As a clear example of its major benefits, I detailed the soon to be rolled out pharmacogenomic programs that will introduce psychiatry to precision medicine, as a major step forward in personalized psychiatry; choosing the right medication for the right patient, at the right time. Raising the important question of whether artificial intelligence can secure and save the future of psychiatry, my affirmative response is that it can, but not alone. Similar advances need to also be brought in from several other related scientific disciplines, such as sociology, psychology, philosophy, ethics, etc.

Overall, such an aspired future is already present, not only in medical sciences, but in our daily life; from the internet to paying electronic bills, from the organization of medical practice to enhancing neuroimaging interpretation, etc. For psychiatry, apart from the most promising pharmacogenomics and precision psychiatric diagnoses, it is hoped that advanced information technology can help in detecting biomarkers to enhance the development of various new conceptual models for psychotherapy. In other words, such advances in information technology can strengthen the scientific basis of psychiatry, which has otherwise been mostly lacking and eroding the role of the psychiatrist. It is gratifying that a few months ago, the Royal College of Physicians and Surgeons of Canada endorsed its council recommendation requiring the integration of information technology and digital approaches to medical practice and the training curriculum in all medical specialties. It is a bold and progressive decision. Not only is this major endorsement by RCPSC the right decision in correctly interpreting the path for the future of medicine, but it supports my decision over a year prior to choose this subject as the main theme of this book.

Continuing with my interest and concern about the future of psychiatry, this book also includes several essays about other important controversies and issues that are grouped into the two categories of phenomenological and nosological challenges, as well as a third category that includes clinical controversies. The essays cover such topics as the subjective/objective dichotomy in psychiatry, the lack of adequate training in neurology and the recent development of behavioural neurology in relation to our old neuropsychiatry. The other category of clinical controversy includes several topics that cover issues such as the recent revival of psychedelics, the fear of taking medications or vaccines and the poorly understood nocebo concept, as well as the issue of whether physicians can practice ethically in defiance of medical science and medical consensus. In the end, by sharing my thoughts and experiences with you, the readers, my best hope in developing this book is to create a broad and serious conversation, with the purpose of securing and saving a strong future for psychiatry.

BIBLIOGRAPHY

Books Consulted

Awad, AG et al: Evaluation of Quality of Care in Psychiatry. Pergamon Press 1980

Gaebel W., Awad A.G: Prediction of Neuroleptic Treatment Outcome in Schizophrenia – Concepts and Methods. Springer-Verlag 1994

Moussaoui D: A Biography of Jean Delay – Excerpts Medica. WPA 2002

Siegel Daniel J.: The Mindful Brain. W.W. Norton & Company 2007

Robinson Ken: Out of Our Minds, Learning to be Creative. Wiley, UK 2011

Kurzweil Ray: How to Create a Mind, The Secrets of Human Thoughts Revealed. Penguin Books 2012

Cozolino Louis: Neuroscience of Human Relationships, Attachments and the Developing of the Social Brain (2nd Edition). W.W. Norton & Company 2014

Tailor Kris: The Patient Revolution – How Big Data and Analytics are Transforming the Healthcare Experience. Wiley 2016

Awad AG, Voruganti LNP: Beyond Assessment of Quality of Life in Schizophrenia. Adis/Spring 2016

Ofri Danielle: What Patients Say, What Doctors Hear. Beacon Press 2017

Pollan Michael: How to Change Your Mind – What the New Science of Psychedelics Teaches us about Consciousness, Dying, Addiction, Depression and Transcendence. Penguin Press 2018

De Vries Glen: The Patient Equation – The Data Driven Future of Precision Medicine and the Business of Healthcare. (The Precision Medicine Revolution in the Age of Covid-19 and Beyond) Wiley 2020

How ChatGPT Works: The Model Behind the Bot by Molly Ruby –towardsdatascience.com
April 23, 2023

Awad AG: The Search for a New Psychiatry. iUniverse, USA 2021

Perakslis Eric D, StanleyM: Digital Health: Understanding the Benefit-Risk Patient-Provider Framework. Oxford University Press 2021

Epstein M: The Zen of Therapy: Uncovering a Hidden Kindness in Life. Penguin Books 2022

Jones Chris: The Eye Test: A Case for Human Creativity in the Age of Analytics. Hachette Book Group, US 2022

Lewis Michael: The Premonition, W.W. Norton, US 2021

Soyer Emre, Hogarth Robin: The Myth of Experience. Hachette Group, US 2020

Robinson Ken: Out of Our Minds, Learning to be Creative. Wiley, UK 2011

Selected Bibliography

Chapter 1 – Starting From Where I Stopped

Awad AG. The Search for a New Psychiatry – On Becoming a Psychiatrist, a Clinical Neuroscientist and Other Fragments of Memory. iUniverse, Bloomington, IN, USA 2021

Ibid. The Political, Social and Economic Environment I Grew Up In, In Egypt (p1-8), Colonial Psychiatry and How It Deliberately Delayed the Development of Academic Psychiatry in Egypt (p27-30), Early Roots of Mental Healthcare in Egypt (p24-26)

Ibid. Face to Face with Endemic Pellagra and Pellagic Madness (p47-51), Reflections on the Issue of Placebo Response (p52-55)

Ibid. My Moscow Years (p63-83), Living in an Atheist Society – Reflections on Science and Religion (p82-88)

Ibid: The Final Stop, Toronto, Canada (p112-144), The Lakeshore Psychiatric Hospital – The Hospital Built by its Patients (p112-117)

Ibid. Quality of Care in Psychiatry (p147-159)

Ibid. Psychiatric Outcomes (p160-171)

Ibid. Current Psychiatric Practices (p175-204)

Hager Thomas. Ten Drugs: How Plants, Powders and Pills Have Shaped the History of Modern Medicine. Abrams Publishing 2019

Tignor Robert. Modernization of British Colonial Rule in Egypt: 1882-1914. Princeton Legacy Library 2016

Keller Richard. Madness and Colonization: Psychiatry in the British and French Empires 1800-1962. Oxford University Press 2001

Foucault Michel. Madness and Civilization: A History of Insanity in the Age of Reason. Vintage Books 1961

Schdlowski M et al. Neuro-Bio-Behavioural Mechanisms of Placebo and Nocebo, Implications for Clinical Trials and Clinical Practice. Pharmacological Review 2015, 67: 697-731

Zubovitch G. Russia's Journey from Orthodoxy to Atheism and Back Again. Danforth Centre in Religion and Politics, Washington University at St. Louis 2018

Engel George L. The Clinical Application of Biopsychosocial Model. American Journal of Psychiatry 1980, 137: 535-544

Selye Hans. Stress and the General Adaptation Syndrome. British Medical Journal 1950, 17:1383-1392

Awad A George. The Neurobiology of Comorbid Drug Abuse in Schizophrenia and Psychotic Disorders, Preedy Victor (ed). Neuropathology of Drug Addictions and Substance Misuse. Vol 1, Elsevier Inc. 2016: 82-88

Awad A. George. The Patient at the Centre of Patient-Reported Outcomes. Expert Review of Pharmacoeconomics and Outcomes Research 2015, 15: 29-31

Voruganti LNP, Awad AG. Subjective and Behavioural Consequences of Striatal Dopamine Depletion in Schizophrenia: Findings from In-vivo SPECT Study. Schizophrenia Research 2006, 88:179-186

Awad AG, Voruganti LNP. Neuroleptic Dysphoria, Comorbid Drug Abuse in Schizophrenia and the Emerging Science of Subjective Tolerability – Towards a New Synthesis. Journal of Dual Diagnosis 2005, 1:83-89

A George Awad. The Concept of Quality of Life in Schizophrenia from an "Ethereal Entity" to a Valued Health Outcome. Journal of Psychosocial Rehabilitation and Mental Health (editorial) 2016, 3:51-52

A George Awad. The concept of Wellness in Psychiatric and Substance Use Disorders, in: Waguih Ishak (ed) The Handbook of Wellness Medicine, Cambridge University Press 2020, p57-65

Chapter 2 - But Then the Covid-19 Pandemic Hit Hard – Necessity Brings Opportunity

Michie Jonathan. The Covid-19 Crisis and the Future of the Economy and Economics. The Review of Applied Economics 2020, 34:301-303

Schippers Michaela. For the Greater Good? The Devastating Ripple Effect of the Covid-19 Crisis. Frontier Psychology 2020, DOI:10.3389/fpsyg.2020.577740

LoGiudice Steven H et al. Overcoming the Covid-19 Crisis and Planning for the Future. The Journal of Nuclear Medicine 2020, 61:1096-1101

Chapter 3 - The Science and Technology Behind the Development of the New mRNA Covid-19 Vaccine – Why it is Relevant to Psychiatry

Shapsin Steven. The Scientific Revolution. University of Chicago Press 2018

Perskalis Eric, Ginsburg Geoffrey. Digital Health: The Need to Assess Benefits, Risks, Provider Network and Values. JAMA 2021, 325:127-128

Brunn Matthias et al. The Future is Knocking: How Artificial Intelligence Will Fundamentally Change Psychiatry. Academic Psychiatry 2020

Chapter 4 - Artificial Intelligence (AI)

Martinho A et al: A Healthy Debate: Exploring the Views of Medical Doctors on the Ethics of Artificial Intelligence. Artificial Intelligence in Medicine, 212 Nov 2021, 102190

Fox Richard. Information Technology: An Introduction for Today's Digital World. Chapmans Hall 2020

Frick Eric. Information Technology Essentials. Frick Industries, Volume 1 2020

Lawton Robert Burns. The Business of Healthcare Innovation. Cambridge University Press 2020

Mowafa Househ et al. Big Data, Big Challenges – A Healthcare Perspective, Background Issues, Solutions and Research Directions. Springer Nature 2019

IBM Cloud Learn Hub. What Is Artificial Intelligence (AI) 2020

Yu KH, Beam AI, Kohane IS: Artificial Intelligence in Healthcare. Nat Biomed Eng 2018, 2:719-731

Davenport Thomas, Kalakota Ravi. The Potential for Artificial Intelligence in Healthcare. Future Health J. 2019, 6:94-98

Koriuek Anton. Why We Need a New Agency to Regulate Advanced Artificial Intelligence: Lessons on AI Control From the Facebook Files. Brookings December 8, 2021

Goldfarb Avi, Teodoridis Florenta. Why is AI Adoption in Healthcare Lagging? Brookings March 9, 2022

Morley Jessica et al. The Ethics of AI in Healthcare: A Mapping Review. Social Science and Medicine 2020, 260:113-172

Johnson KB et al. Precision Medicine, AI and the Future of Personalized Healthcare, Clinical and Translational Science. https://doi.org/10.1111/cts.12884 2020

Kalis B et al. 10 Promising AI Applications in Healthcare. Harvard Business Review, May 10, 2018

Reddy S et al. A Governance Model for the Application of AI in Healthcare. Journal of the American Medical Informatics Association 2020, 27:491-497

Nording Linda. A Fairer Way Forward for AI in Healthcare. Nature September 2019, 573, issue775

Hague DC. Benefits, Pitfalls and Potential Bias in Healthcare AI. North Carolina Medical Journal 2019, 80:219-223

Naylor David. On the Prospects for a (Deep) Learning Healthcare System. JAMA 2018, 320:1099-1100

Abbimanyu S Ahuja. The Potential for Machine Learning-Based Wearables to Improve Socialization in Teenagers and Adults With Autism Spectrum Disorders. JAMA Pediatr. 2019, 173:1105-1106

Shimonski Robert. AI in Healthcare: How Artificial Intelligence is Changing IT Operator and Infrastructure Services

Jackson Philip C. Introduction to Artificial Intelligence. Dover Publication Inc., NY 2019

Muller Vincent C. Philosophy and Theory of Artificial Intelligence. Springer Science and Business Media 2012

Kissinger Henry et al. The Age of AI and our Human Future. Little Brown 2021

Castano AP. Machine Learning, Bots and Agent Solutions. Apress Media 2018

MIT Technology Review. Are Psychiatrists Really Ready for the AI Revolution. August 27, 2019

Fakhoury Marc. Artificial Intelligence in Psychiatry. Springer Nature 2019

Ducharme Jamie. How AI Could Save Psychiatry, Artificial Intelligence Could Help Solve America's Impending Mental Health Crisis. Time, November 20, 2019

Marc Fakhoury. Artificial Intelligence in Psychiatry. Advances in Experimental Medicine and Biology 2019, 1192:119-125

Bateman Kayleigh. Four Ways Artificial Intelligence is Improving Mental Health Therapy. World Economic Forum, December 22, 2021

Martin Max. Artificial Intelligence Helps Improve Outcomes for Depression Treatment. First of Its Kind Clinical Trial Shows Benefits of AI for Mental Healthcare. Western News December 8, 2021

Jagoo Krystal. Artificial Intelligence Could Be the Future of Mental Illness Detection. Very Well Mind January 24, 2022

Fielding Sarah. For Better or Worse, Technology is Taking Over the Health World. Very Well Mind September 29, 2021

Series Peggy. Computational Psychiatry. MIT Press 2020

Bush Ryan A. Designing the Mind: The Principles of Psychitecture. Designing the Mind 2021

Pham Kay T et al. Artificial Intelligence and Chatbots in Psychiatry. Quarterly 2022, 93:249-253

Blease C et al. Artificial Intelligence and the Future of Psychiatry: Qualitative Findings from a Global Physician Survey. Safe Digital Health 2020

Chapter 5 - The Current State of Artificial Intelligence in Medicine and Psychiatry, and the Reasons for Low Interest Among Psychiatrists

Graham Sarah et al. Artificial Intelligence for Mental Health and Mental Illnesses: An Overview. Curr Psychiatry Rep 2019, 21:116

Stewart Jonathon E et al. Medical Specialties Involved in Artificial Intelligence Research: Is There a Leader? Tasman Medical Journal 2020, 2:20-27

Malik P, Rathur VK. Overview of Artificial Intelligence in Medicine. J Family Med and Primary Care 2019, 8:2328-2331

Benjamen S et al. The State of Artificial Intelligence-Based FDA Approved Medical Devices and Algorithms: An Online Database. npi Digital Medicine, Open Access, September 11, 2020

Hinton G. Deep Learning Technology with the Potential to Transform Healthcare. J Am Med Assoc 2018, 320:1101-1102

Doraiswamy Murali P et al. Artificial Intelligence and the Future of Psychiatry: Insights from a Global Physician Survey. Artificial Intelligence in Medicine 2020, 102, #101753

Blease C et al. Artificial Intelligence and the Future of Psychiatry: Qualitative Findings from a Global Physicians' Survey. Digital Health 2020, Volume 6, October 27

Lee Ellen E et al. Artificial Intelligence for Mental Health Care: Clinical Applications, Barriers, Facilitators and Artificial Wisdom. Biological Psychiatry: Cognitive Neuroscience and Neuroimaging 2021, 6:856-864

Sprujt-Metz D et al. Extended Abstracts of the 2022 CHI Conference on Human Factors in Computing Systems. Association for Computing Machinery, New York, USA, Online April 28, 2022

Mamykina L et al. Grand Challenges for Personal Informatics and AI. Ibido, April 2022, pages 1-6

Chen ZS et al. Modern Views of Machine Learning for Precision Psychiatry. Scopus, Elsevier, April 4, 2022

Frances Allen. Future of Psychiatry in a Post-Pandemic World. Psychiatric Times, June 4, 2020

Summer Allen. Artificial Intelligence and the Future of Psychiatry. EMB, May/June 2020

Nijs MG, Bueno de Mesquita JM. The Future of Psychiatry and the Psychiatrist of the Future. Tigdschr 2019, 61:217-223

Nasrallah Henry. Psychiatry's Future is Here: Here are 6 Trends that will Fundamentally Change Psychiatry. Academic Psychiatry 2020, 44:416-466

Brunn M et al. The Future is Knocking: How Artificial Intelligence Will Fundamentally Change Psychiatry. Academic Psychiatry 2020, 44:416-466

Reznick RK in collaboration with Council Task Force on Artificial Intelligence and Emerging Digital Technologies. Task Force Report on Artificial Intelligence and Emerging Digital Technologies. RCPSC February 2020

Office of The Privacy Commissioner of Canada. A Regulatory Framework for AI: Recommendations for Personal Information Protection and Electronic Documents Act (PIPEDA) Reform, November 12, 2020

Canadian Institute for Advanced Research. AI and Healthcare: A Fusion of Law and Science – An Introduction to the Issues, Toronto 2021

Harwich Eleonara, Laycock Kate. Thinking on Its Own: AI in the NHS. info@reform.uk

Joblin Anna et al. The Global Landscape of AI Ethics Guidelines. Nature Machine Intelligence 2019,1:389-399

Government of Canada. Canada's Scientists Encouraged to Pitch Projects that Bridge Artificial Intelligence. Health Research – News Release, June 13, 2018

UNESCO, Recommendation on the Ethics of Artificial Intelligence. https://en.unesco.org;ethics

Bowen Julie. What Psychiatrists Think About Artificial Intelligence. https://arxiv.org/abs/1907.12386 August 6, 2019

Scheetz J et al. A Survey of Clinicians on the Use of Artificial Intelligence in Ophthalmology, Dermatology, Radiology and Radiation Oncology. Scientific Reports, 11, number 5193, 2021

Pinto Dos Santos D et al. Medical Students' Attitudes Towards Artificial Intelligence: A Multicentre Survey. Eur Radiol April 29, 2019, 4:1640-1646

Chapter 6 – Artificial Intelligence and Predictive Strategies in Psychiatry

Awad AG. Prediction Research of Neuroleptic Treatment Outcome in Schizophrenia – State of the Art: 1978-1993 in W Gaebel and AG Awad (eds) Prediction of Neuroleptic Treatment Outcome in Schizophrenia, Concepts and Methods. Springer-Verlag, Vien 1994

Ceskova Eva, Silhan Petr. From Personalized Medicine to Precision Psychiatry? Neuropsychiatr Dis Treat 2021, 17:3663-3668

Salazar de Pablo G et al. Implementing Precision Psychiatry: A Systematic Review of Individualized Prediction Models for Clinical Practice. Schizophrenia bulletin 2021, 47:284-297

van Shaik Ron HN et al. Pharmacogenetics in Psychiatry: An Update on clinical Usability. Front Pharmacol September 11, 2020, Frontierin.org

Winter Nils R, Hahn Tim. AI and Machine Learning for Precision Psychiatry: How Are They Changing the Clinical Practice? Fortschr Neurol Psychiatr 2020, 12:786-793

Butler Merlin G. Pharmacogenetics and Psychiatric Care: A Review of Commentary. J Ment Health Clin Psychol 2018, 2:17-24

Menke A. Precision Pharmacotherapy: Psychiatry's Future Direction in Preventing, Diagnosing and Treating Mental Disorders. Pharmgenomics Pers Med 2018, 11:211-222

Bzdok D, Myer-Lindenberg A. Machinge Learning for Precision Psychiatry: Opportunities and Challenges. Bid Psychiatry Neurosci Neuroimaging 2018, 3:223-230

Kennedy J, Virelli C. Pharmacogenomics in Psychiatry: A Brief Overview. ca.editorial@mediaplanet.com

Riehter Thalia et al. Machine Learning-Based Behavioral Diagnostic Tools for Depression: Advances, Challenges and Future Directions. J Pers Med 2021 Oct, 11(10):957

Martinho A et al. A Healthy Debate: Exploring the Views of Medical Doctors on the Ethics of Artificial Intelligence. Artificial Intelligence in Medicine 2021, 121; November 2021, 102190

Chapter 7: Imagining Psychiatry in the Era of Artificial Intelligence and Big Data

Zarley B. David. Meet the Scientists Who Are Training AI to Diagnose Mental Illness. The Verge.com, January 28, 2019

Rocheteau Emma. On the Role of Artificial Intelligence in Psychiatry. Brit J Psychiatry, Cambridge University Press, Sept 12, 2022, 1-4 (online)

Chandler Chelsia et al. Improving the Applicability of AI for Psychiatric Applications Through Human-in-the-loop Methodologies. Schizophrenia Bulletin 2022, 48:949-957

Simon GE, Yarborough BJ. Good News: Artificial Intelligence in Psychiatry is Actually Neither. Psychiatric Services, 2020, 219-220, January 8, 2020 (on line)

Wiese W, Friston KJ. AI Ethics in Computational Psychiatry, From the Neuroscience of Consciousness to the Ethics of Consciousness. Behav Brain Res Feb 26, 2022, 420, #113704

Chapter 8: The Big Question: Can Artificial Intelligence Deep Machine Learning and Big Data Analytica Save the Future of Psychiatry?

The Big Question: Can Artificial Intelligence, Deep Machine Learning and Big Data Analytica Save the Future of Psychiatry?

Mesko Bertlan. The Future of Psychiatry: Telehealth, Chatbots and Artificial Intelligence. The Medical Futurist, August 26, 2021

Chapter 9 - Neuropsychiatry, Behavioural Neurology and the Inevitable Meeting of Minds – Towards a New and Unified Field of "Clinical Neuroscience"

Arciniegas DB, Anderson AC, Filley CM (editors). Behavioural Neurology and Neuropsychiatry. Cambridge University Press 2013

Sachdev PS, Mohan A. Neuropsychiatry: Where Are We and Where Do We Go From Here? Mens Sana Monograph 2013, 11:4-15

Benjamin S. Educating Psychiatry Residents in Neuro-Psychiatry and Neuroscience. Int Rev Psychiatry 2013, 3:266-275

Silbers Weig D, Safar LT, Daffner KR. Neuropsychiatry and Behavioural Neurology, Principles and Practice. McGraw Hill 2021

Breedlove SM, Watson NV (editors). Behavioural Neuroscience. Oxford University Press 2019

Kazamel M. The Split Between Neurology and Psychiatry: Historical Review. Neurology (15 Supplement) Online ISSN:1526-632X, 2022 American Academy of Neurology

Fitzgerald M. Do Psychiatry and Neurology Need a Close Partnership or a Merger? BJP Bulletin 2015, 39:105-107 and online by Cambridge University Press January 2, 2018

Keshavan SM, Price BH, Martin J. The Convergence of Neurology and Psychiatry – The Importance of Cross-Disciplinary Education. JAMA 2020, 324:544-555

Butchart L. Cross-Training in Neurology and Psychiatry. JAMA 2020, 324:2557-2558

Pies RW, Daly R. Should Psychiatry and Neurology Merge as a Single Discipline? Psychiatric Times Vol 27, No. 3, March 4, 2010

Martin JB. The Integration of Neurology, Psychiatry and Neuroscience in the 21st Century. Am J Psychiatry 2002, 159:695-704

Reynolds EH. Structure and Function in Neurology and Psychiatry. Br J Psychiatry 1990, 157:481-490

Price Bruce, Adams Raymond, Coyle Joseph. Neurology and Psychiatry – Closing the Great Divide. Neurology 2000, 54:8-14

Chapter 10 - The Subjective/Objective Dichotomy – Relevance to Nosology, Research and Clinical Practice

Awad AG, Voruganti LNP. The Subjective/Objective Dichotomy in Schizophrenia – Relevance to Nosology, Research and Management, in: W. Gaebel (ed) Zukunftperspektiven in Psychiatrie und Psychotherapie 2002, ps. 21-27, Springer Verlag Heidelberg 2002

Awad AG. Subjective Response to Neuroleptics in Schizophrenia. Schizophrenia Bulletin 1993, 19:609-618

Awad AG, Hogen TP, Voruganti LNP, Heselgrave RJ. Patient Subjective Experiences on Antipsychotic Medications: Implications for Outcome and Quality of Life. Int Clin Psychopharmacology 1995, (suppl 3) 123-132

van Praag HM. Reconquest of the Subjective. Brit J Psychiatry 1992, 160:266-271

Voruganti LNP, Heselgrave RJ, Awad AG. Neuroleptic Dysphoria May be the Missing Link Between Schizophrenia and Substance Abuse. J Nerv and Ment Disease 1997, 185:463-465

Strauss JS. Subjective Experiences of Schizophrenia: Towards a New Dynamic Psychiatry. Schizophrenia Bulletin 1989, 15:178-179

Husserl E. Experience and Judgment. North Western University Press, Evanston, Ill., USA 1973

Awad AG, Voruganti LNP, Heselgrave RJ, Hogan TP. Assessment of the Patient's Subjective Experiences in Acute Neuroleptic Treatment: Implications for Compliance and Outcome. Int Clin Psychopharmacol 1996, 11:55-59

Fonzi Laura et al. Exploring How the Psychiatrist Experiences the Patient During the Diagnostic Evaluation: The Assessment of Clinician's Subjective Experiences (ACSE) Phenomenology and the Cognitive Sciences 2022, 21:107-119

Chapter 11 - Lunacy and the Moon – Reflections on the Interactions of the Brain and the Environment

Arkowitz H, Lilienfeld – Lunacy and the Moon – Does a Full Moon Really Trigger Strange Behaviour? Scientific American (MIND), February 1, 2009

Geddes Linda. The Mood-Altering Power of the Moon. BBC Future, July 31, 2019

Golembiewski Kate. Why Do We Still Believe in "Lunacy" During a Full Moon? Discover, August 16, 2019

Clark Tim. Does the Moon Make People Crazy? Almanac, September 12, 2022

Conut Maria. Can the Moon Really Influence Your Health? Medical News Today, August 9, 2013

Foster RG, Roenneberg T. Human Responses to the Geophysical Daily, Annual and Lunar Cycles. Curr Bid 2008, 18:R784-94

Chapter 12 - "Woke Psychiatry"! What Is It?

Ungar Thomas. "Woke" Psychiatrists Have Lost Sight of the Biological Causes of Mental Illness. The Globe and Mail, Toronto, October 9, 2021

Tarico Valerie. An Excess of Woke Thinking May Harm Mental Health or Relationships, posted on December 15, 2021

Nacoste Robert. To Be or Not To Be "Woke". Psychology Today, Canada, posted September 29, 2019

Salel Sally. How Psychiatry Has Gone Woke and Other Troubling Developments in Science. YouTube, January 22, 2022

Ferguson CJ. Scientific Institutions Are Going Woke – and Hemorrhaging Credibility. Opinion New Week, September 14, 2022

Chapter 13 - The Ignored Uncommon Psychiatric Disorders and the "Herd" Pattern of Psychiatric Research Interests

Pommepuy N, Janwel D. Catationia Resurgence of a Concept. A Review of the International Literature. Encephale 2002, 28:481-92

Tang VM, Duffin J. Catatonia in the History of Psychiatry: Construction and Deconstruction of a Disease Concept. Prospect Bid Med 2014, 57:524-537

Ellul P, Choucha W. Neurobiological Approach of Catatonia and Treatment Perspectives. Front Psychiatry 2015, Online December 24, 2015, 6:182

Edinoff AN et al. Catatonia: Clinical Overview of the Diagnosis, Treatment and Clinical Challenges. Neural Int 2021, 13:570-586

Chapter 14 - Notes on Creativity, Emotions and Psychiatric Disorders

Andreasen N. The Relationship Between Creativity and Mood Disorders. Dialogues Clin Neurosci 2008, 10:251-255

Waddel C. Creativity and Mental Illness: Is There a Link? Can J Psychiatry 1998, 43:166-172

Andreasen NC. Creativity and Mental Illness: Prevalence Rates in Writers and Their First Degree Relatives. Am J Psychiatry 1987, 144:1288-1292

Flaherty Alice. Frontotemporal and Dopaminergic Control of Idea Generation and Creative Drive. J comparative Neurology 2005, 293:147-153

Crabtree J et al. Anxiety and Adverse Life Events in Professional Creative and Early Psychosis Population. Psychiatry 2020, 83:328-343

Davis Mark. Understanding the Relationship Between Mood and Creativity: A Meta Analysis. Organizational Behaviour and Human Decision Processes 2003, 108-25-38

Abraham Anna. The Neuroscience of Creativity. Cambridge University Press 2018

Vartanian Oshin, Bristol Adam. Neuroscience of Creativity. MIT Press 2013

Jung RE et al. The Cambridge Handbook of the Neuroscience of Creativity. Cambridge Press 2018

Sample I. New Study Claims to Find Genetic Link Between Creativity and Mental Illness. The Guardian, June 8, 2015

Skillicorn N. What is Creativity? Definition, History and Science. Idea to Value, May 24, 2021

Chetan Walia. A Dynamic Definition of Creativity. Creativity Research Journal 2019, 31:237-249

Chapter 15 - Loneliness; The Invisible and Silent Disorder

Mann F et al. Loneliness and the Onset of New Mental Health Problems in the General Population. Soc Psychiatry and Psychiatric Epidemiol 2022. https://doi.org/10.1007/s00127-22-02261-7

Morr M et al. Chronic Loneliness: Neurocognitive Mechanisms and Interventions. Psychother Psychosom 2022, 91:227-237

Cacioppo JT, Patrick W. Loneliness. Norton & Co 2008

Cacioppo Stephanie, Cacioppo John. Introduction to Social Neuroscience. Princeton University Press 2020

Bzdok D, Dunbar R. The Neurobiology of Social Distance. Trends Cogn Sci 2020, 24:717-733

Zajner C et al. Loneliness is Linked to Specific Subregional Alterations in Hippocampus-Default Networks Covariation. J Neurophysiol 2021, 26:2138-2157

Lam JA et al. Neurobiology of Loneliness: A Systematic Review. Neuropsycho-Pharmacology 2021, 46:1873-1887

Achterbergh L et al. The Experience of Loneliness Among Young People with Depression: A Qualitative Meta-Synthesis of the Literature. BMC Psychiatry 2020, 20:1-23

Chapter 16 - The Fear of Taking Medications – The Nocebo Concept

Colloca L, Barsky AJ. Placebo and Nocebo Effects. N Engl J Med 2020, 382:554-561

Weimer K et al. Placebo and Nocebo Effects in Psychiatry and Beyond. Front in Psychiatry, August 7, 2020

Faisse K et al. Experimental Assessment of Nocebo Effects and Nocebo Side Effects: Definitions, Study Desgin and Implications for Psychiatry and Beyond. Front in Psychiatry, June 14, 2019

Matthews A et al. Impact of Statin Related Media Coverage on Use of Statins: Interrupted Time Series with UK Primary Care Data. BMC 2016, 353:i3283

Benedetti F. The Need to Investigate the Nocebo Effects in More Detail. World Psychiatry 2019, 2:227-228

Mestre TA, Lang Anthony, Odun M. Factors Influencing the Outcome of Deep Brain Stimulation Effects: Placebo, Nocebo, Lessebo and Lesion Effects. Mov Disord 2016, 3:290-296

Benedetti F et al. The Need to Investigate the Nocebo Effects in More Details. World Psychiatry 2019, 2:227-228

Mestre TA et al. Factors Influencing the Outcome of Deep Brain Stimulation Effects: Placebo, Nocebo, Lessebo and Lesion Effects. Movement Disorder 2016, 3:290-296

Chapter 17 - Prolonging Illness Behaviour and the Contribution of Ruminative and Clinging Behaviours

Kirmayer L, Looper KJ. Abnormal Illness Behaviour: Physiological, Psychological and Social Dimensions of Coping With Distress. Cur Opin Psychiatry 2006, 19:54-60

Epstein Mark. The Zen of Therapy, Uncovering a Hidden Kindness in Life. Penguin Books 2022

Chapter 18 - The Past is Coming Back as The Future – The Rise, Fall and the Rise Again of Psychedelics

Doblin RE et al. The Past and Future of Psychedelic Science: An Introduction To This Issue. Psychoactive Drugs 2019, 51:93-97

Aday JS et al. Beyond LSD: A Broader Psychedelic Zeitgeist During the Early to Mid-Twentieth Century. J Psychoactive Drugs 2019, 51:210-217

Carhart-Harris RL, Goodwin GM. The Therapeutic Potential of Psychedelic Drugs: Past, Present and Future. Neuropsychopharmacology 2017, 42:2105-2013

Lowe H et al. Psychedelics: Alternative and Potential Therapeutic Options for Treating Mood and Anxiety Disorders. Molecules 2022, 27:2520

Reiff CM et al. Psychedelics and Psychedelic-Assisted Psychotherapy. Am J Psychiatry 2020, 177:391-410

Sherman J. Five Important Events in Psychedelic History, Psychtech-Psychedelic Education, January 31, 2021

Eskin Tessa. Ketamine:The Chemistry, Effects and Brain Science. PSYTECH, April 2, 2021

Pilecki B et al. Ethical and Legal Issues in Psychedelic Harm Reduction and Integration Therapy. Harm Reduct J 2021, 18:40

Chapter 19 - Alternative Medicine Versus Alternative "To" Medicine – Reflections on the Blurry Line Between Science and Commercialism

Ratini Melinda. What Exactly is Alternative Medicine? Web MD, March 20, 2021

Astin John. Why Patients Use Alternative Medicine – Results of a National Survey. JAMA 1998, 279:1548-1553

National Centre for Complementary and Integrative Health and NIH. Complementary, Alternative or Integrative Health: What's in a Nam. https//www.nccih.nih.gov.health

Awad AG. The Concept of Wellness in Psychiatric and Substance Use Disorders, in: Ishac W: The Handbook of Wellness Medicine. Cambridge University Press 2020

Hoffer A. Adventures in Psychiatry – A Scientific Memoirs. KOS Publishing Inc. 2005

Chapter 20 - Can Physicians Ethically Practice Against Science and Mainstream Medical Consensus?

Drescher J. Physician Values and Clinical Decision Making, Commentary. AMA J Ethics, May 2006

Gorski D. The Covid-19 "Vaccine Holocaust", The Latest Antivaccine Messaging. Science-Based Medicine, May 10, 2021

Doshi P. Covid-19: Spreading Vaccine "Misinformation" Puts License at Risk, US Boards Tell Physicians. BMJ 2021, 375:n24717

Kunzelman M. Anti-Vaccine Doctor Sentenced to Prison for Capitol Riot. Toronto Star/The Associated Press, June 16, 2022

Novella S. The Ethics of Deception in Medicine. Science-Based Medicine, January 23, 2008

Chapter 21 - Aging and Its Many Impacts

Awad AG, Voruganti LNP. Family burden of Care in Schizophrenia – A Review. Pharmacoeconomics 2008, 26:149-162

Sethumadhaven A, Saunders M. Aging: Looming Crises or Booming Opportunity? World Economic Forum, March 18, 2021

Lawrence RM, Head JH. Aging. Published online by Cambridge University Press, January 2, 2018

Sykes T. Aging and Mental Health – A Forgotten Matter. Mental Health Europe, September 1, 2014

Fernandes L, Paul C. Aging and Mental Health, Editorial. Front Aging Neurosci 2017, 9:25

World Health Organization. Aging and Health, Consultation on Global Strategy and Action Plan on Aging and Health, 2015

CBC News. New Census Figures Showing Aging Population Pose Future Problems for Canada, Experts Warn, April 27, 2022

In Praise of:
"The Search for a New Psychiatry" by A. George Awad.
Published by iUniverse, Bloomington, USA, July 21,2021

The Search for New Psychiatry,
by George Awad, iUniverse 2021

This is an engaging, informative, and important book about the problems inherent in the current practice of psychiatry. Written by an experienced, internationally renowned psychiatrist, it calls for a new perspective on what is needed to heal mental/emotional disorders. The author sees psychiatric practice through a historical and global lens, well acquainted with the benefits and hazards of psychopharmacology and the hope and limits of shifting psychotherapeutic methods. It is a personal book, which details the author's journey, geographic and philosophical, through a complex series of conceptual ideas in psychiatry as applied, or misapplied, today.

Mary V. Seeman
Professor Emerita, University of Toronto
Toronto, Canada

Narrative skills are an essential part of psychiatric theory and practice. Some psychiatric scholars (e.g., Sigmund Freud and Oliver Sacks) relied on keen observation while others (Victor Frankl) meditated on their lived experience in enriching psychiatry. Professor Awad weaves a gripping story of his trans-continental journey both as an Alien and an Alienist during the most rapid phase of expansion of psychiatry as a scientific discipline and as a clinical specialty in the post-war era of reverse colonization and globalization.

His personal story of inter-faith, inter-generational and international turmoil and triumph juxtaposed with the scientific, political and socio-cultural developments during the psychopharmacology revolution offers a rink-side seat to the microcosm of Canadian psychiatry over the past 50 years.

This book is an essential read to enhance cultural sensitivity among Psychiatry residents and also a reassuring companion for all international medical graduates.

> Lakshmi N.P. Voruganti, MD, MSc, Ph.D.
> Halton health Care, Oakville Trafalgar
> Memorial Hospital, Oakville, Canada

Dr. Awad has been a friend and mentor for the past 10 years. Before reading his memoir however I was not aware of the details of his life or his great skill as a writer. He tells a very compelling and inspiring story of his life in Egypt and then of his life in psychiatry in Toronto. His writing to me personifies the concept of "medical humanism", in both bringing rigorous scientific thought as well as humanity to the study of medicine and psychiatry in particular. I hope this book will be widely read both because it challenges us to think more clearly about psychiatry and for its inspiring example of a life well lived.

> Sameer Kumar MD FRCPC
> Staff Psychiatrist, Humber River Hospital

Excerpt from a Book Review: Springer Nature "Journal of Psychosocial Rehabilitation and Mental Health" 2022; 9: 123-124

This book of about 230 pages makes very interesting reading, and for people who are in the early part of their career, they can imagine that it is how they might end up after they finish forty or fifty years of practice of psychiatry. The book is very interesting because it reflects the history of the development of psychiatry, as well as personal experience through the eyes of a very knowledgeable and experienced psychiatrist who has put his lifetime experience in this book.

The book is interspersed with "gyan" about life, like his observation that unplanned events can turn out to be much better than planned ones; an experience which may give comfort to those who find that things are not working out as planned or expected...

This affordable book is a must-read for all students of psychiatry and behavioural science, as well as mental health. The book would be an important addition to the collection of the books in libraries not only in psychiatric institutions but also in medical colleges.

Professor Santosh K. Chaturvedi
Leicestershire University, UK
Editor-in-Chief of Springer Nature:
"Journal of Psychosocial Rehabilitation &
Mental Health"

ABOUT THE BOOK

This book is the second in the series I began in 2021, with the publication of the book "The Search for a New Psychiatry"

My extensive reflections and analysis of the state of the art of modern psychiatric practices, based on my own experiences over the past fifty years and supplemented by similar observations and conclusions by a number of expert colleagues, both senior or in the middle of their careers, all point to the inevitable conclusion that modern psychiatric practices have failed many: patients, their families, doctors and society at large.

Patients and their families continue to struggle with ineffective and lengthy treatments that are at best only partially effective. Psychiatrists are quickly feeling burnt out by the lack of a strong science to back their practices, and their psychiatric progress does not proceed in a straight line by being frequently interrupted with long stagnant periods separating the few peaks of scientific progress. The society at large is concerned with the rising costs, on the face of relatively poor or limited outcomes. Altogether, as concluded in my 2021 book, there is clearly a need for a new and more effective psychiatry. It was at this point that the book ended, with an appeal for different ways to secure the important future for psychiatry.

This book takes over from where the 2021 book stopped, and now a new dialogue has begun regarding the promising approaches in psychiatric care with which to save and secure the future of psychiatry. Such important reforms are highly needed, starting with the challenging question of whether rapidly evolving modern informatics, including such developments as artificial intelligence and big data analytics, can secure the future of psychiatry, as has recently happened in some medical fields, such as imaging, immunology and others. This book briefly provides an overview, in terms of the rapid development in information science and technology and what it can contribute to psychiatry, including its limitations and risks, as recently demonstrated in the very rapid development of Covid-19 vaccines.

In Part Two, the book also provides a number of other clinical, phenomenological and nosological challenges that have been forgotten or not yet resolved. The list includes such topics as Behavioural Neurology versus Neuropsychiatry and whether both can be merged into a new sub-specialty such as Clinical Neuroscience. Other important topics include a critical review of "The Past is Coming Back as the Future: The Rise, Fall and the Rise Again of Psychedelics". The rapidly evolving question of "Aging Gracefully, Really?!" is also reviewed, as well as other unfolding modern challenges. At the end is a post-script about the recent death of a close friend and a major pioneer in psychoneuropharmacology, Tom Ban.

Part Three provides an extended Bibliography and list of recent books that proved helpful and critically informative in accessing other opinions and valuable experiences.

BOOKS PUBLISHED BY THE AUTHOR

- Evaluation of Quality of Care in Psychiatry,
  Pergamon Press 1980

- Disturbed Behaviour in the Elderly,
  Pergamon Press 1987

- Prediction of Outcome to Neuroleptic Therapy in Schizophrenia –
  Conceptual and Methodological Issues,
  Springer Verlag, Vienna 1994

- Quality of Life Impairment in Schizophrenia, Mood and Anxiety
  Disorders,
  Springer 2007

- Beyond Assessment of Quality of Life in Schizophrenia,
  Adis/Springer 2016

- The Search For a New Psychiatry,
  iUniverse, USA 2021

ABOUT THE AUTHOR, IN HIS OWN NARRATIVE

Dr. A. G. Awad

Dr. Awad is a Professor Emeritus in the Department of Psychiatry and is on the Faculty of the School of Graduate Studies at the Institute of Medical Science, University of Toronto, Canada

In 1949, I enrolled in medical studies at the Faculty of Medicine, Cairo University, Egypt. Throughout my six years of medical undergraduate studies, Cairo and other major cities were besieged by major political upheaval, including frequent massive demonstrations that at that time had led to violence and the assassination of politicians. The economy was failing, moving from one crisis to another and was further crippled by rising religious extremism. Among the major events that led to the temporary disruption of regular life and suspension of schools and university studies, was the humiliating defeat of the ill-prepared Egyptian army in 1948, in the Israeli War of Independence in Palestine.

In January 1952, Cairo was besieged by massive demonstrations that lead to the torching of the centre of Cairo, including all foreign and, specifically, British-owned fashion and entertainment businesses, in what is known as Black Saturday. This major incidence was triggered by the massacre of over fifty Egyptian police officers in the city of Ismailia, beside the Suez Canal, by British army forces camped around the canal, under the false pretense that the police officers were preparing to attack the British garrison nearby. In six months, amidst the political unravelling in Cairo and other big cities, the Egyptian army seized power, abandoned the corrupt monarchy, toppled the government and assumed full political and governmental power in what became known as the "July 23rd Revolution".

About four years later, in 1956, the year that was assigned to be the graduation of our medical class, all of a sudden the country was besieged by an abrupt and rather complex disquieting event known as the Suez Crisis, that quickly impacted several aspects of regular life, including the postponement of my graduation until the following year. The Suez Crisis began with what started as an ambitious plan to deal with major economic disparities between the failing agricultural sector and big-city economies, through the construction on the Nile of one of the world's largest embankment dams, the Aswan High Dam. It was to provide year-round water for expanded agricultural purposes and for further generations of electricity, to enhance the electrification plans of the countryside outside big cities. It was good and encouraging news for Egypt, but President Nasser and his government had to secure massive economic support for such a major project from the United States, the United Kingdom and other wealthy countries.

However, in early 1956, the United States and other countries started to express displeasure with President Nasser's evolving close relationship with the Soviet Union and its allies for the procurement of modern military weaponry. With President Nasser ignoring such threats and becoming more critical of western countries meddling in Egyptian internal policies, in no time the conflict turned into a major crisis, with the United Kingdom and the United States threatening the suspension of the funding plans of the Aswan High Dam. The crisis became further deepened by the rise of the western powers' concerns about Nasser's overambitious political influence in the Middle East. By mid-1956, with the failure of the negotiations, the western countries announced the suspension of the funding agreement.

In an angry and retaliative response, President Nasser announced the seizure of the Suez Canal management, in a major speech given on the fourth anniversary of the 1952 army revolution. Management of the canal had been imposed by western countries shortly after its opening in 1863, as the result of concerns about massive foreign debts incurred during the construction of the canal and the extra lavish expenditure incurred by the Ottoman/Egyptian ruler, Khedive Ismail, in the opening celebrations of the canal. The highly secretive arrangement by the United Kingdom, France and Israel to seize back the management of the Suez Canal by force seemed to quickly fade away and eventually failed, as a result of the massive protests critical of the return of the colonial era, as well as the United States' negative response for not being consulted about the Tripartite Invasion and the fear of precipitating a much bigger conflict and war with the Soviet Union. In the end, President Nasser was clearly the winner, reclaiming the ownership of the canal. As a result, he was emboldened to continue his expansive and aggressive international plans, threatening neighbouring countries.

On the other hand, the Suez Crisis, in personal terms, turned out to be a major negative turning point for my future plans and my life in general. My early arrangements for further post-graduate studies in London, as was frequently done by Egyptian medical graduates, was abruptly cancelled as a result of the suspension of all relationships between the UK and Egypt, in the aftermath of the failed Suez Canal invasion. The only alternative was to accept my first independent job, an assignment as a rural physician serving a rather poor and remote region of Egypt, close to the Suez Canal and the extensive British camps that held the British garrison that continued their occupation of Egypt.

My three-year medical service in the impoverished region of Bani Ayoub, turned out to be the best experience for a young physician early in his/her medical career. Successfully fighting pellagra, a major endemic nutritional deficiency condition, brought quick fame to me and conferred on me almost magical and mystical powers. The noted lack of energy and the tiredness and lethargy of pellagra's victims, including common serious dermatological skin changes, as well as the more serious central nervous-system complications that led to cognitive deficits such as dementia, began improving in a matter of less than six months of treatment with vitamin and nutritional supplements, such as inexpensive Baker's yeast and its rich vitamin B complex, which seemed to clearly make a major gradual recovery that looked like a general "awakening".

As often noted, success and fame brings more success and further fame. Word of my local popularity eventually reached and impressed my superiors in Cairo, who declared my medical program in Bani Ayoub a resource for the field testing of new medications. An added responsibility was quickly established to test the very new and soon to be approved contraceptive pill, donated by an American international foundation interested in social engineering in over-populated, but underdeveloped countries. Our quickly established contraception clinic, without any fanfare nor much publicity in order to avoid antagonizing religious local authorities, proved to be an immediate success, most likely as a result of a small monetary added reward for the patients of ten piastres. A new focus was on the emerging and significant socioeconomic problem of the rapidly increasing population in Egypt, although, with its sparse population, it was not a significant challenge in the region I was serving.

Nevertheless, the new focus brought me closer to my continuing interest in academic medicine, by seconding me on a part-time capacity basis to join Professor Fouad Al-Hifnawi, to assist him in developing a new academic program concerning reproductive biology and population growth, at the recently developed National Research Centre in Cairo. Back in the region of Bani Ayoub the program proved to be a success by the number of women enrolled, though in my opinion the program was a mixed success, as a significant number of women were observed dropping the pills in the river on their way home from the clinic, despite my continuous urging of my superiors in Cairo to introduce a medication education and support program. Nevertheless, my academic interests and the popular recognition I received finally softened my long maintained resistance of going to Moscow for postgraduate training, to equip myself for an academic future at the National Research Centre in Cairo.

By the end of January 1961, I was already in Moscow and starting what I used to call "the expedition into the unknown", by which I meant the language barrier and the political, cultural and ideological differences that by and large were not very familiar to me. In spite of the major inconveniences in daily life, I enjoyed a good deal of support from my supervisor, Professor Youssef Abramovitch Eskin, and all forty-two of his female scientists in the Department of Experimental Biology, at the Institute of Experimental Endocrinology. My research and clinical focus was on the exploration of the new concept of "stress" on health and illness, as elaborated at that time by the most popular breakout concepts of Professor Hans Selye, at McGill University in Montreal, Canada. My almost four years in Moscow ended successfully in earning me a PhD degree, and is best described as a good mix of curiosity of the Soviet Union and its system, major struggles with daily living hardships, conflicts with ideology, though I was exempted from any formal ideological studies, occasional feelings of loneliness and being in a completely different environment. Nevertheless, I managed to develop extracurricular interests, such as the role of religion and, more precisely, its mandated absence in the progress of science. In an extensive informed exploration, I reached the uncontested conclusion that the absence of a formal religion did not impact on scientific progress, as such, except that in the Soviet Union the benefits from science were not equally distributed among the population, but was more focused on military and political targets and sectors.

Returning back to Cairo at the end of 1964 proved to be a major disappointment, as a result of my mis-appointment to direct a toxicological program, testing urgently imported grain. Weekly ships brought grains to the port of Alexandria, where supposedly random samples were sent to my laboratories in Cairo for biological clearance, by testing it on mice that were fed different doses of grains for different periods of time. It didn't take long for me to quickly realize the limitations of such primitive testing of grain, which was open in its lengthy and uncontrolled travel from Alexandria to Cairo and possibly subject to external manipulations, including being used for potential significant bribes. All efforts to reform the procedure failed, for fear of creating delays in the provision of government-subsidized bread and the subsequent possibility of loud protests. In the end, I was frustrated with the wasteful waiting game of receiving a response from the several applications I had sent to various health institutions in Europe, seeking a post-doctoral post that could guarantee an exit permission from Cairo. Fortunately, in a few months it happened.

By early 1968, I was already established in Rome's internationally well-known Institute for Health Research, meeting with my supervisor, Professor Ameliocardi Carpi, and his academic research assistant, Dr. Carla Cartoni, having been offered a welcomed plan to continue my research interests in the concept of "stress" by joining Dr. Cartoni, who was about to start a major research project regarding "cardiovascular reactivity to stress". My experiences included working in Professor Cartoni's program of pharmaceutical chemistry and, in general, at the well organized international institute, as well as being close to many other important research laboratories, particularly that of Professor Rita Levi-Montalcini, who later was awarded the Nobel Prize for Physiology. Overall, work there proved to be very enjoyable and friendly. That atmosphere was in high contrast to the outside environment at the centre of Rome, where the daily violent protests by the "Red Brigade" and the frequent protest clashes of other anarchist groups took place, and sadly on one occasion led to the assassination of Prime Minister Aldo Moro. By the fall of 1968, the research project was completed and results tabulated, and a manuscript had been provisionally accepted for publication in the European Medical Journal, "Pharmacodynamics and Therapy".

With such a successful conclusion of my post-doctoral year, the other looming challenge left was what to do and where to go, since I had decided not to return to Cairo. By shear coincidence, a friend and colleague from Prague, Dr. Karel Cocandrle, contacted me. He, like myself, was holding a post-doctoral Fellowship from the same institution in Rome, and had interrupted his studies in Rome by accepting an offer from the Canadian government for all Czech citizens who desired to immigrate to Canada to be granted immediate status, in the aftermath of the Russian Army invasion of Czechoslovakia. He and his wife settled in Edmonton, Alberta, where he was accommodated at the University there. In a short time, he connected me with the Professor of Endocrinology at the soon-to-open medical school in nearby Calgary, Alberta, at the University of Calgary. After several phone calls and exchanges of documents, within a few weeks I had accepted his offer to join him and committed to the development of a new laboratory for experimental neuro-endocrinology. It was a sudden and great relief, but not without concern about Calgary's frigid winter weather, which was somewhat similar to what I had endured in Moscow. Nevertheless, it was a great offer that enabled me to achieve my desire to settle in an academic career. However, as had happened before, similar to my previous plan of going to London in the aftermath of the Suez Canal crisis, Calgary all of a sudden was not to be my destination.

During a short stop for a few days in Toronto, before continuing on to Calgary, I was offered an academic research position in the Department of Pharmacology at the University of Toronto. Unplanned, and what I considered to be an opportunity to develop contacts to serve future purposes in Calgary, I decided to visit the University of Toronto campus. My only contact there was that of the late Professor Edward Schoenbaum, whom I had met at a conference in Rome. In a few minutes, Professor Schoenbaum introduced me to Professor Edward Sellers, the head of the Department of Pharmacology and serving as the Associate Dean of the medical school at U of T. In less than an hour, I immediately accepted his offer to join the Department of Pharmacology, with a commitment to deal with a major "thyroid" multi-centre and stalled research project. Up to the present time, and after almost fifty years, I continue to be puzzled by my unusual and immediate acceptance of such an unintended and sudden proposal in Toronto. Could it have been just expediency in following the principle of "A bird in the hand...", or possibly it was just the perfect alignment of meeting the right person in the right place and at the right time?

In two years the thyroid research project was resurrected, completed and a paper submitted to the well-known medical journal, The Lancet, and accepted for publication. A major accomplishment that also proved to be a time for reflection and a desire to move to a clinical field, which can be more secure and economically more supportive, particularly as I had started a bit too late in my medical and academic career in Canada. Not wanting to wait too long, I received rather quick and generally unexpected advice from the late Professor Harvey Stancer, who used to attend our weekly thyroid meetings. He suggested I move to the Department of Psychiatry, which at the time was building strong interest in psychobiology, replacing the waning psychoanalytic dogma. Once more, the idea was appealing, represented by the noticeable peak of research interest in the neurosciences at that time.

To hold a clinical post, I had to get a medical license to practice and spend few years in a residency training program. Fortunately, this requirement was reduced to a little over two years, in consideration of my previous research experience and PhD work. This was then another twist in my career, and my time as a senior psychiatric resident passed rather quickly; one year at the Clarke Institute of Psychiatry in the Clinical Investigation Program, supervised by both Professor Harvey Stancer and Professor Harvey Moldofsky, and the second year was spent at a major psychiatric hospital still popularly known as "999 Queen Street West" in Toronto, supervised by the late Professor Sebastian Littman. Dr. Littman deepened my interest in the clinical management and research of schizophrenia and psychotic disorders, and introduced me to British psychiatrists, such as Kurt Schneider and Karl Jaspers. Additionally, I received supervision by the late Professor Alexander Bankalo, who introduced me to phenomenology and neuropsychiatry.

By 1974, I was ready and qualified to start my first independent clinical job in Canada, at the old Lakeshore Psychiatric Hospital. It was recognized as the only hospital built by its patients, who were long-term patients that came from the other overcrowded provincial psychiatric hospital, the well-known "999 Queen Street West". In less than two years, I moved to 999 Queen Street West to assume a senior service and academic post, which ushered in the next fifty years of my life as a psychiatrist and neuroscientist, and continued my research interests in schizophrenia and psychotic disorders. I also moved between senior academic and clinical administrative roles, including serving as a Professor of Psychiatric Research, as well as the Psychiatrist-in-Chief at Wellesley and St. Michael's Hospitals, and more recently at Humber River Hospital in Toronto, which included the merger of three general hospitals. I also served in several national and international organizations.

In Canada, I made several contributions to the Canadian Psychiatric Research Foundation (CPRF), serving as Chair of its Professional

Committee and as a member of the Board of Directors Committee. For a number of years I served as the editor of the monthly publication "Bulletin of the Canadian Psychiatric Association" (CPA). In 1994, I was elected as the ninth President of the Canadian College of Neuropsychopharmacology (CCNP). More recently, I served as the first founding president of the International Society of CNS Clinical Trials Methodology (ISCTM). My extensive international experience included several contributions to such organizations as the International Collegium of Neuropsychopharmacology, the International College of Geriatric Psychopharmacology (ICGP), the National Institute of Mental Health (NIMH) and the National Institute of Aging, among several other professional and scientific organizations.

I was honoured to receive recognition and several awards that included the Joey and Toby Tannenbaum Family Award for Distinguished Scientist in Schizophrenia Research and the CCNP medal for meritorious contributions in psychopharmacology research, teachings and services. More recently, I received the Andrew C. Leon Distinguished Career Award for my contributions to the Foundation of ISCTM.

As well, I've been recognized for extensive research contributions that focused on the person behind the illness and advocated for patient-centred care, broadening concepts such as quality of life, wellness and well-being. During my thirty-year study with colleagues of why several patients with schizophrenia disliked and almost hated to take their antipsychotic medications, we uncovered for the first time the origin of dopamine functioning in the striatal region of the brain, which clarified why many patients on antipsychotics take to concomitant substance use and abuse. Meanwhile, I maintained significant clinical and research interests focused on systems and quality of psychiatric care, as well as the burden of care on the family. I also contributed several book chapters, major reviews and several published books, including my most recent book, "The Search for a New Psychiatry", published in 2021 by iUniverse in USA.

I am proud to have trained several generations of psychiatrists and graduate students, and am most appreciative of the many colleagues who joined my research teams over the past fifty years, in particular Drs. Lakshmi Voruganti and Ronald Heslegrave, who made several long-term important contributions over the years. Major credit also needs to go to our patients and their families, who trusted us and shared their inner sufferings and challenges in support of our research efforts, with the hope for us to be more helpful to others.

Dr. A. G. Awad
dr.a.g.awad2@gmail.com

Printed in the United States
by Baker & Taylor Publisher Services